PRAISE FOR

Arise and Shine

"If you've ever wondered if your life makes a difference amid the darkness of our world, this book is for you. *Arise and Shine* is the practical guide you need to stop questioning your purpose and instead give the gift God has graciously placed within you. Through three stages, Allyson beautifully leads us to uncover, unleash, and unapologetically shine the light this dark world is desperate for. No more wondering or hiding; it's time to shine!"

—ASHLEY MORGAN JACKSON, bestselling author of
Tired of Trying, speaker, and writer for Proverbs 31 Ministries

"This book is a beacon of light in a world where it often feels like darkness and brokenness are all around us. If you're discouraged, *Arise and Shine* will equip and uplift you in truth. Each page is saturated with words of wisdom and hope."

—JORDAN LEE DOOLEY, national bestselling author of
Own Your Everyday and *Embrace Your Almost*

"*Arise and Shine* is a worthy message for our generation. Through her testimony and the power of Scripture, Allyson pulls our focus off the darkness and onto the true Light who walks with us every day. If you're feeling discouraged or dimmed by this world or your circumstances, *Arise and Shine* will be your guide."

—TARA SUN, author of *Surrender Your Story* and host of
the *Truth Talks with Tara* podcast

"Allyson has created an amazing book that will help you find joy in your everyday as you seek God's presence. Her heart shines through her stories, and her biblical teaching will make you feel seen and empowered to shine your light."
—GRACE VALENTINE, @thegracevalentine, bestselling author

"I love that Allyson is such a light to this generation. Through her words and gifts, she points people to the light of Christ. *Arise and Shine* will leave you feeling encouraged and empowered to live connected to the source of light and to be the hands and feet of Jesus in a broken, lost world. Filled with the truth of God's Word and encouragement on every page, you will not want to put this book down!"
—ASHLEY HETHERINGTON, YouTuber and founder of
the Honey Scoop

ARISE AND SHINE

ARISE AND SHINE

How to Be the Light That Ignites Hope in a Dark World

ALLYSON GOLDEN

Foreword by Madison Prewett Troutt

WATERBROOK

Details in some anecdotes and stories have been changed to protect the identities of the persons involved.

Published in the United States by WaterBrook, an imprint of Random House, a division of Penguin Random House LLC.

Book design by Caroline Cunningham
Title font styling by Micah Kandros, font sourced from Shutterstock
Title page and part title background art: iStock/Ariel Design, boxed text art: iStock/meen_na

Nana and Papa, Mom and Dad,
your light ignited the light within me.

My sweet husband, Michael,
you've helped keep the light in me aflame when
the Enemy wanted to put it out.

Arise, shine, for your light has come,

> and the glory of the LORD rises upon you.

See, darkness covers the earth

> and thick darkness is over the peoples,

but the LORD rises upon you

> and his glory appears over you.

—Isaiah 60:1–2

FOREWORD

STATISTICS SHOW THAT ALMOST three in five girls report feeling sad or hopeless almost every day, and nearly 30 percent of teen girls reported in 2021 that they seriously considered suicide.[1] A hopelessness epidemic is happening around us, and for many of us, it's happening inside of us. We're wrestling with thoughts like, *How did I get here? Where are You, God? Do You even care? What's the point of living?*

For me, the lies, the darkness, the hopeless feelings that nothing will ever change have ruled over my mind more times than I can count. A few of those phases include getting cheated on, being taken advantage of sexually, feeling betrayed by a best friend, being stuck in a job I hated, feeling ridiculed on live television, getting bullied and canceled on social media, walking through suffering with someone I love, and losing a loved one. I have had many seasons of doubt, discouragement, and deep darkness.

I know what it's like to feel stuck. I know what it's like to believe the lies. I know what it's like to be bound by the darkness of shame and fear. I'm guessing you picked up this book because you do too. (Cue "We're All in This Together" from *High School Musical.*) Just like I did, you will feel comforted and encouraged in reading this book, that no matter where you are in your faith journey, no matter what you are battling, you are not alone.

Has anyone ever asked you, "Do you want the bad news or good news first?" Well, I am going to give you the bad news first: *This world is broken and dark.* Okay, now to the good news: *Jesus is light.* I found the Light. And you can too. You can find a glimpse of hope and search for light amid your darkness. You can break free from the lies and walk in the freedom and light that God has for you. And this book can be that first step!

When Allyson and I met at a Christian retreat in December 2020, I immediately knew there was something different about her. She had a fire in her eyes, a big smile packed with joy, and peaceful and composed confidence. I felt, *This girl has probably never had a bad day in her life!* We didn't get to spend a lot of time together at this retreat, but I began following her on social media because I had to know more about her. She shared on social media some of the dark days she was experiencing, low moments she was walking through, and the hope and truth she clung to amid it all. I was so encouraged by her vulnerability and the way she encouraged others with her own pain. It was so evident her heart was surrendered to Jesus and that the light within her was much bigger than her.

When she reached out and asked me to write this foreword, I was honored and excited to play even a small part in this message. As I began reading this book, I was challenged and convicted. I texted her, "This message is full of hope and truth. I needed this!" Not only is this a message I need to be reminded of constantly, but also it is a message for you—and for everyone. In our world today, it's easy to believe the lies of the Enemy, follow the cravings and passions of our flesh, and fall prey to conforming to the culture around us. In following the lies, ourselves, or even culture, we are left hopeless and confused. This book will point you back to the Light, the Truth, and the only One who can overcome and defeat the lies and darkness we all feel and face.

In this book, Allyson shares her experiences and story with humility, vulnerability, and authenticity. You will feel as if you are sitting across from her having coffee, realizing, *Oh she has had bad days too!* If you desire to break free from hopelessness and confusion and sin, grow in your faith, and walk out your purpose, this book is for you. If you desire to be bold in your beliefs and convictions, this book is for you. Not only will you be challenged in your faith, but you also will be inspired to take what you receive and experience to others.

Arise and Shine will encourage your heart and challenge your thinking. You will walk away from reading feeling empowered, equipped, and excited to live a life connected to the Light and ready to bring that light to others. You—yes, *you*—now have a purpose and a calling to rise up, know the truth, and share that truth. This book, filled with God's Word, will remind you that it is the Lord alone that causes your light to shine!

For You cause my lamp to be lighted and to shine; The LORD my God illumines my darkness. (Psalm 18:28, AMP)

—MADISON PREWETT TROUTT, bestselling author of
Made for This Moment and *The Love Everybody Wants*

CONTENTS

PART I

DIMMED LIGHT

At one time you lived in darkness. Now you are living in the light that comes from the Lord. Live as children who have the light of the Lord in them.

—Ephesians 5:8, NLV

1

WHERE IS THE LIGHT?

An Introduction

I WILL NEVER FORGET that night. Even though I was a trained pediatric nurse, no class or person could have prepared me for what happened.

During my drive to the hospital that evening, I prayed that God would guide me as I worked. I had just hit my year-and-a-half mark, so I was still a relatively new nurse. I prayed for a good patient assignment because, let's be real, no nurse ever wants to have a hard shift.

As I took the elevator to my unit, I continued to ask God to equip me for the night. The first thing I typically do is head to the nurse's station, sit down at a computer, and look at the whiteboard that has the nurses' names next to our assigned patients. When I wrote down the room numbers of my patients, I noticed my name next to a patient who had been on the unit for many months. In most hospitals, nurses can request to be assigned to long-term patients since continuity of care is nice for the nurse and the patient. However, I had never requested this patient and had taken care of him only once before. I looked around the station and noticed there were other nurses on duty who *had* requested this patient but had not been assigned to him, but I didn't say anything.

I jotted down pertinent information from the computer about all my patients onto the piece of paper nurses call our "brain," which I would carry around during my twelve-hour shift. I went into each of my patients' rooms, took their vitals, gave them their meds, reviewed the plan of care with them, and then began to do my charting. The last one on my rounds was the long-term patient. I knew he had gone through some really hard things. He was getting better physically but, unbeknownst to me, was still struggling emotionally. I didn't know him well, so when I was in his room, I didn't sense that anything was off. I gave him his medications at eight o'clock and left to allow him to get a good night's sleep. However, around eleven o'clock, his call light beeped. *He probably just has a headache and wants some Tylenol.*

When I opened the door to his room, an eerie silence greeted me. The lights were off, and as I flipped the switch on, I asked, "Is there anything I can get you? I saw that you called the nurse's station." I pulled the curtain back, and my heart leaped out of my chest as I realized that he had attempted to end his life and must have pushed the call button accidentally (or changed his mind) right before he passed out. I yelled for help and checked to make sure he still had a pulse. A co-worker ran in, realized what was going on, and called for more help. We initiated a code blue to get the ICU team to come quickly and continued to do everything we could to save him. By the grace of God, he lived and was okay.

As everything began to calm down, I walked out of the patient's room and . . . I lost it. I realized that *I* was not okay. I could not believe what had just happened. I was hyperventilating. I could hardly get words to come out of my mouth, but the tears would not stop flowing. Another nurse took me into our break room so that I could have some space to try to pull myself together. I could tell I wouldn't be able to finish the shift. The charge nurse told me that I could go home, and my amazing co-workers took over my patients. I reached for my phone to call my husband and prayed that he would hear it ring. It was midnight, and I knew that driving home alone was not a good idea. When I heard him answer, I could hardly speak to ask him to come get me.

As I began to process what had happened, I couldn't help but question: *Why would this patient want to end his life? Why is there so much darkness in the world? And why was I assigned as his nurse that night, of all nights? Why me, God? What was the purpose in this?*

Unfortunately, this near disaster was not an isolated situation. Frontline workers and nurses like me see tragedy daily. Left unchecked, emotional stress can wear us down.

Several months after the episode with the patient who tried to take his own life, I was feeling worn down. As five o'clock hit one night and it was time to get up for work, I could barely get myself out of bed. It had been another rough shift the night before—this time with a different patient—and I had a hard time motivating myself to get up and do it all over again. I managed to brush my teeth, put on my scrubs, and throw my hair up in a bun. I headed downstairs to the kitchen where my husband had dinner on the table, along with my lunch packed and ready to go. I struggled to thank him because I was stuck in a negative mindset and didn't want to go back to the place where darkness loomed and negativity brewed.

I left the house with my backpack on, lunch in one hand and coffee in the other, anticipating the eight-minute drive to turn into at least fifteen minutes with the good ole Southern Califor-

nia traffic. As I got in my car, I took a deep breath and pressed
the button on my steering wheel to call my mom. I often called
her on my way to work, especially when I needed to vent.

"Hi, Mom. Whatcha doin'?"

She answered, "Oh, your dad and I just sat down to eat some
salmon. Are you on your way to work?"

"Yes, and it is the last place I want to be right now," I responded.

"I'm sorry, Allyson. How did you sleep, and how was your shift
last night?" my mom asked.

"I slept well, but the shift was really rough."

Always keeping the confidentiality of my patients in mind, I
shared that I had taken care of a new patient who seemed to be
losing hope. This girl was feeling lonely, lost, and frustrated because so much was now out of her control due to her paralysis.

I said, "On top of all the things I have to do for my other patients, I feel like I need to support this girl because she has no
family or friends at her bedside. I'm trying to encourage her, but
it's hard when I'm feeling so discouraged myself."

My mom responded, "I am so sorry. I'm sure you were exactly
what your patient needed."

How do I give God my burdens? How do I keep going?

"Thanks, Mom. Not only did I have that patient to take care
of, but we had admissions come in from the emergency depart-
ment that were non-accidental traumas. It's so hard to see life-
and-death situations, especially knowing that so many doctors,

nurses, and families of these patients don't know Jesus. I feel like I'm doing my best to keep myself together. But again, last night, I had to step outside to get some fresh air. It all just feels too heavy. And the hospital is short-staffed right now, so nobody has a good attitude."

"That's hard. I'll be praying for your shift that the Lord will strengthen you to do what He has called you to do. Go and be a light tonight."

What? Be a light? Has she been listening? That is the last thing I feel like doing right now. How in the world can there be any light in this situation? How can I be a light to others when I feel overwhelmed by the darkness? It was too much. I had enough going on in my life. I had so many things to focus on while I was at work, and the negativity was constant. It felt impossible to be a light. However, instead of voicing my thoughts, I just said, "Okay, I'll try. Thanks, Mom. Love you. Talk to you later."

What about you? Does it ever feel impossible to be a light when your own life and circumstances are consumed with darkness and hardship? It seems like every day we are exposed to heart-shattering, life-altering, hard-to-process grief and suffering. Whether it is actively happening in our own lives or the lives of people we know, pain digs its way deep down into our hearts and lingers, producing an overwhelming, inescapable feeling of darkness. It's like walking down a road on a cold night with no streetlights, no front porch lights, and clouds covering the light of the stars. We can't see what's in front of us, yet we know we have to keep going.

At this point in my life, the brokenness of the world weighed heavily on my shoulders. I felt like I had to carry everything I was experiencing at work, the weight of my own pain, and the pain of loved ones all on my own. I found it hard to release my burdens to God; I didn't know how to hand over what I was feeling to Him. People often say, "Give God your burdens," but all I could think was, *How do I do that? How can I stop feeling this way?* I felt that if one more burden was placed upon my shoulders, I would collapse and shatter into a million pieces. I questioned, *How do I keep going? How do I push through?* My mind and heart felt so overwhelmed.

Asking these questions scared me. I immediately thought that I wasn't a strong enough Christian and that people would judge me for questioning. I feared others would look at me and think I was a phony. But these feelings were real. These were true questions that I asked myself and God. I realize now that I allowed myself to believe the lie that I shouldn't verbalize these thoughts and feelings. I questioned, *Why am I choosing to hide? Why are we not talking about these hard questions and how to live life amid the crises that surround us?*

Maybe this is where you are too. You feel weighed down by the shattering brokenness of the world or the temptations of the Enemy. Are you unsure how to give God your burdens? Are you questioning God's purpose for where He has you or what has happened to you? Do you feel alone in your questioning? You may desire to shine the light of Jesus but wonder how to do that when you struggle to see the light yourself, just like I did. How can we be lights for Jesus in a world that is consumed with darkness and led astray by the Enemy? How can we be lights while yearning desperately for the hope that Jesus's light brings for ourselves?

Well, my friend, I promise you that you're absolutely not alone. As I write this, I am thinking of you. I am so sorry. If I could sit across from you at coffee, I would reach out and give you a big hug. You've got a sister right here who sees and feels the pain you're dealing with. We could talk and share stories and tears, but

I wouldn't let you leave our coffee date feeling like you are trapped in the darkness. Because, in fact, that is a complete lie from Satan. He comes to steal, kill, and destroy our hope, and he does everything he can to make us feel like light doesn't exist. And truly, it is so easy to believe the lies of the Enemy. His voice can seem louder than our own voice and even God's voice. But, my friend, no amount of darkness, absolutely no plans of the Enemy, can overcome the light that is within Jesus. Wherever God has you right now, He is with you. His light is within you. And He is so eager to shine through you like only He can. And we're going to be talking a lot more about that in the pages to come!

I would be doing a disservice to the calling God has placed on my life if I were to let you walk away feeling like you were trapped in that darkness. So, since we cannot have an in-person coffee date, grab your favorite drink (I have mine!), and let's go over some truths together as you read this book. We are going to wrestle with the questions above. We will find answers to some and realize that for others, we will have to hold on to our faith tightly because we won't know the answers on this side of heaven. What I can tell you is that this book is going to equip you for moments when you feel unable to shine God's light. Your eyes will be opened to new ways of looking for light. By the end, you will be shining brighter than ever, and His light will be undeniably radiant everywhere you go, within you and around you.

My hope and prayer is that you will feel inspired and ignited to go and do what you have learned.

This book is sectioned into three parts. In these first few chapters, we are going to hit on the real and raw feelings we experience as humans here on earth. I believe in the power of validating and sitting with our feelings. Feelings were created by the Lord for a reason. Don't let this scare you away. My friend, I know you have some things you need to let yourself feel. I know that I certainly do. But as we move from the first part of this book into the second, you will not be left alone in your feelings. The second part is where the equipping will happen. While feelings are important, they aren't facts, and we can't let our feelings get in the way of the fullness the Lord has for us. The second part is where we will dive deep into God's Word, learn what the Bible says about light, and discover how we can tangibly apply His Word to our lives. As we move from the second part into the third, my hope and prayer is that you will feel inspired and ignited to go and do what you have learned. And not only that but also share it and ignite the light of Christ within others.

At the end of each chapter, there will be a call to action titled "Arise and Shine." These sections will provide you with tangible ways to apply what you have just read. They are filled with to-dos that will hopefully feel exciting for you to complete. After all, my heart in writing this book is for these words to not only take root in your heart but also to spring you forward into action. This world needs hope to be ignited, and you, my friend, will walk away being a light igniter!

So, what do you say? If it seems impossible to be a light for Christ at times, know that I have been there and still have hard moments where light feels hidden. But we are going to take this one step at a time and acknowledge along the way how difficult this journey can be. It isn't something that changes in a moment. It is a lifelong learning process that will ebb and flow with new

experiences. Get ready to stomp on the lies of the Enemy together as we discover and become confident in the truth that the
Lord has spoken over us. Hang with me, friend. I care about you
too deeply for you to stay in a place of darkness. Keep reading to
discover what it means to fully live your calling to be a light for
Christ!

2

LIGHT EXPOSURE

God's Presence Changes Perspective

MONTHS AFTER I BEGAN to recover from the trauma of watching one of my patients attempt suicide, which had been my first experience seeing something extremely dark and scary, I decided that I wanted to seek the Lord in new ways.

I also wanted to see if anyone else was wrestling with the same feelings and questions I had when it came to being a light in this broken and hurting world. I decided to throw out a poll on my Instagram stories. I asked, "Does the darkness of this world or of your past make you feel like it is so hard to find the light or be the light?"

Loads of answers came in saying things like, "Yes, that is me!" or "Definitely!" I was surprised by how many people responded, and I was relieved that I wasn't alone. At the same time, I also felt sad that so many of us were stuck in these feelings and questions.

Even before my patient's attempted suicide at the hospital, I had felt the Lord nudging me to write a book about light, but after seeing the results of the polls, I knew that I *needed* to write it.

This motivated me to begin studying the word *light* in the

Bible. I dove deep into what the Bible says about Jesus being the light of the world and how He calls us to go and be the light. I also researched the sun, the moon, rainbows, stained-glass windows, kaleidoscopes, mirrors, and many other objects in which light plays a part. I started to interview friends and ask them questions about how they have experienced the light of Christ in their own lives.

The Lord's revelations during this time were mind-blowing. As I went about my days, He would show me something about Himself through the way I perceived light. I began to see the world through a new lens, a lens I believe we all have access to. This book shares what I learned during that time of deep study. And now anytime I hear something that has to do with light in any form, I get giddy. (Ask my husband—it's pretty comical sometimes.) My sincere prayer is that this will also happen to you as the Lord speaks to you through this book!

LIGHT IS NOT HIDDEN

So why did I choose to share with you one of my darkest days as a nurse? It's because I bet you have had difficult situations in your life where you questioned God's purpose. He isn't placing those things in your life to tear you down. Rather, He wants you to fulfill your purpose by being a vessel of His light to this very dark world.

He wants you to fulfill your purpose by being a vessel

of His light to this very dark world.

Maybe you're thinking you aren't strong enough, bold enough, or capable enough to carry His light. But, my friend, you are. In fact, He has chosen you specifically to be a light in dark places and in hard spaces where no one else wants to go—where, at times, you might not want to go either.

Maybe you have a grueling job like I do. Or you might be weighed down from something in your past. Maybe you're in the middle of a broken relationship or you come from a broken family. Maybe you have experienced the death of a loved one, had a miscarriage, or been hurt by others and feel isolated. Maybe you are struggling with a mental illness that feels all-consuming, or you're fighting an addiction. Maybe you are harboring a secret that no one knows about. Maybe you have had suicidal thoughts or attempted to end your own life.

Perhaps these things listed above have caused you to ask such questions as:

- *Where is the light?*
- *Is the darkness ever going to go away?*
- *How can I be a light when I struggle to see it?*
- *Can Jesus shine through me when I feel like this?*
- *Why would Jesus want to shine through someone like me?*
- *When I do discover the light, how do I hold on to it?*
- *What do I do if I can't find the light?*

These questions are so real. They are all things I have asked myself. But rest assured, God doesn't expect you or me to be "strong enough" on our own. He doesn't expect us to know exactly what to do when the darkness floods our minds or know the correct answers to all our questions. He wants to show us His loving grace that lives in the tension we feel when we ask Him hard questions.

I don't know about you, but I want to be a person who brings hope to others. I want to be full of joy and be a bright shining light for Jesus. But there are some days when it feels too hard to see the light through the dark circumstances in my path. I wish that the darkness didn't exist. I wish it was easier. I long for the day when there will be no more darkness.

We are told in the Bible that we are going to face trials, but so often the ones I'm facing feel too heavy and too hard to bear. It feels easier to stop searching for the light and to quit persevering through the trials. I can feel weary and burnt out from the darkness that consumes my mind and heart. It seems as if there isn't a way out. Even though I know God calls me to place my fears, worries, and questions on His shoulders and He promises to give me rest, I sometimes wrestle with these heavy feelings.

Darkness has a way of telling us that we are stuck. It wants us to feel like it controls us; but the truth is, it doesn't. We have the power to choose to let the darkness control us or take control of it ourselves with God's help. The Enemy wants us to believe the lie that there can't be light amid darkness. Satan doesn't want us to have the hope that Jesus brings us. Satan uses things in this fallen world to blind us from the truth. But we are going to learn how to stand confident in the full truth of who Jesus is!

DARKNESS CANNOT OVERCOME LIGHT

Now, three years later, when I reflect on the night of my patient's attempted suicide, I can't help but notice how the Lord was intertwined throughout the entire situation. For some crazy reason, God chose me to be his nurse that night. The other nurses who normally took care of him were all busy at the time the call light came on, but I was able to go right away. I don't even want to imagine what would have happened if there had been a delay in response because his nurse was tending to another patient. And while I would never wish for anyone to experience what we did, my co-workers on that shift were the best team I could have asked for, and I know that God handpicked us for that specific night.

John 1:4–5 says, "In him was life, and that life was the light of all mankind. The light shines in the darkness, and the darkness has not overcome it." In other words, Jesus *is* the light of the world. We may feel overwhelmed by darkness, but it will never overcome us because Jesus's light is in us and around us. All the negative or hard things you see on your phone do not have a hold on you. The negativity that may surround you at work cannot get in the way of God's plan for your life. The darkness you see as you go about your day will not overcome you because of the power that is simply in Jesus's name. It might feel hard to believe and see right now because of your circumstances. Discovering how to find the light of Christ and how to *be* it for Him takes time. It is a process, but it's a process you are more than capable of. You are right where you need to be at this moment, and He is with you.

A lot of times we think that "shining the light" means being full of joy, bringing hope and excitement to people, or delighting in happy moments. While I believe light is in those things, I have learned that light shines the brightest in hard situations. Without darkness, we wouldn't know what light is. It is in darkness that light contrasts the most and shines brighter than ever. Just like the light of the sun piercing through the broken pieces of a stained-glass window, Jesus—the light of the world—pierces through our dark, broken pieces and shines through us for all the world to see. There may be darkness in this world, but light breaks through to shatter it.

As I look back now to three years ago, there *was* light the night of the suicide attempt, and it was Christ in me. Christ working amid a very dark and hard situation. I know full well that His presence was in that patient's room, guiding my co-workers and me.

The Bible promises that the light shines in the darkness, and the darkness will *not* overcome it. In the presence of the Lord, absolutely no darkness can overcome His light. And His light is fully within those who believe in Him and who are *focused* on all of who He is. Even in the darkest of situations.

FOCUS ON THE LIGHT

When I was in college, it seemed that everyone had a cool camera and was able to take amazing photos. I did my best to make do with my iPhone camera, but deep down I *really* wanted a nice camera. I'm talking Sony, Canon, or Nikon nice. So, wanting to fit in with the crowd, I began to save some money. A few months passed and I finally had enough to buy the Canon camera I had been eyeing. I was so excited about the photos I was going to take that I even made my own photography Instagram account. (Just trying to fit in with the cool kids, you know?)

I started to watch YouTube videos and taught myself how to use the camera. I studied aperture, f-stop, long exposure, using the manual setting, etc. I found it fascinating, and taking photos soon became my new hobby. I came to realize that I preferred taking photos of nature rather than people. There was something so beautiful and awestriking to me about capturing God's creation. I moved from being a beginner to an intermediate photographer quickly and decided I wanted to attempt taking photos of the stars (back before iPhones had automatic long exposure and could do this).

Back to handy-dandy YouTube I went to study up on the best way to take photos of the stars. I learned that there was something essential I needed in order to do this: a tripod. If you try to take long-exposure photos without a tripod, odds are they will end up super blurry because it's almost impossible for our hands to stay in the same spot for even a few seconds. So, of course, I ordered a tripod right away. My most memorable attempt to get photos of the stars was at my favorite place in the world: Mammoth Mountain, California. I grew up going to Mammoth to ski in the winter and to hike and fish in the summer. The stars were always incredible in the evenings because of the high elevation and the lack of light pollution from nearby cities.

This particular astrophotography trip to Mammoth was during the summer between my freshman and sophomore years of college. I was starting to feel comfortable using the camera in the manual setting and was so excited to finally try to get some amazing star photos. I set up my tripod so it was overlooking a beautiful lake, and I made sure the camera was in focus. I adjusted the settings and increased the ISO (the camera's sensitivity to light) and the f-stop (which partially controls the amount of light that is let into the lens). Finally, I set the shutter speed to seven seconds. Shutter speed plays a huge role in long-exposure photos because it determines how long the lens is open to the light. The photos that came from this shoot were beautiful. It was incredible to see how a camera captured the starlight in what looked like darkness.

So, what does this have to do with spiritual darkness? What I now realize is that we, too, can see light in what appears to be darkness if we hold still and look through a new lens. Just as a tripod holds a camera steady to focus clearly on stars, when we let ourselves sit still in the presence of Jesus—the light—and fix our eyes on Him, we begin to see more than darkness. And just as the camera's slow shutter speed allows in more light, when we slow down, our eyes are exposed to more of His light. It's in this process of focusing and exposing that we begin to see the Lord's perspective of our circumstances. And that's when our mindset shifts.

> Sit with Him, fix your eyes on Him, and expose
>
> yourself to all that He is.

In the chapters ahead, I'm going to explain how this happened to me when I sat still with the Lord, fixed my eyes on His character, and let myself be exposed to the Light Himself. As I looked through a new lens, my perspective shifted, and I was in awe of what was actually around me.

My friend, the Lord wants this for you too. He wants to reveal His light to you right where He has you. But it's going to be hard to see if you aren't fixing your eyes on who He is and spending time with Him. You aren't going to find the light you are searching for in relationships, jobs, social media, vacations, or books. The one true Light you are longing for will be found when you seek Jesus: Sit with Him, fix your eyes on Him, and expose yourself to all that He is.

If you're thinking, *That all sounds great, Allyson, but you haven't told me how to do this,* just hang on. We are going to dive into these things. I will teach you what it means to sit with the Lord, focus on all that He is, and place yourself in His presence.

Please know that I see you and I am with you. I have been there, too, when the circumstances felt too heavy and dark to have any light in them. Let's begin the process of putting a new lens on. Fix your eyes on Jesus and let Him change the way you see things. He is the Author and Creator of all, and He wants you to see things how they really are: already overcome by the Light of the world.

ARISE AND SHINE

- Journal about a time you felt consumed by darkness. (Write what you were thinking, feeling, and experiencing.)
- Now ask the Lord what He wants to tell you about that time, and journal what you feel Him speak to you.
- Read John 1:1–8.
- What is one way you can sit still with, focus on, and expose yourself to the Light this week?

3

HIDDEN DARK BOXES

Bringing into the Light the Things
We Want to Hide

ADDICTION, SIN, SECRETS, PAST TRAUMA, insecurities, and failures. We try to stuff these dark things in a box and hide them where no one can see them. We are afraid that if we bring them into the light, our lives will change—for the worse. Thoughts run through our minds of what people will think or say to us if they "only knew." The Enemy convinces us that if we confess our sin to another person we will be harshly judged, so it is better to bury it and keep it a secret. He persuades us that what other people think is more important than what God tells us. The Enemy wants to keep us trapped and chained to our sin, while the Lord wants to set us free from it.

And when it comes to our desire to be a shining light for Christ, it's easy to feel disqualified when we have a deep, dark secret restricting our heart and mind, constantly reminding us of our hidden sin.

Do you know what disqualifies you from shining the light of Christ? Nothing! No matter how dark you feel your sin is or how broken you think you are, Jesus's love for you is so wide and so deep that even amid your brokenness, He wants to use you to shine His light on others.

My good friend Stacia is the perfect illustration of this. She was a pastor's kid, known by everyone. It seemed like she had what every high school girl wanted, and she even drove a pink truck. (I mean, how fun is that?) Wherever she went, she was the life of the party, and everyone wanted to be her friend. She had a way of making others feel loved and known, so it was no surprise that she had many friends outside of her church as well. From a distance, her life looked very appealing.

But when she was alone, she struggled. When no one was watching and when no one was home, the Enemy subtly turned Stacia's eyes away from Jesus and she became addicted to pornography. The Enemy quietly drew her in and convinced her that watching these videos and looking at photos would satisfy her in a way that nothing else could. She walked around school and lived her life like she had it all together, but inside her secret was tearing her apart.

In the beginning, she didn't feel like she was addicted to pornography. The Enemy would lie to her and say, *You're just educating yourself.* Many of her friends were partaking in sexual sin, so in her mind, she justified her use of pornography as okay because she wasn't actively doing all the things her friends were doing. But it slowly became a cycle. She felt trapped in it, like she would never be able to get out. She felt incredibly alone.

After watching porn, she would feel guilty and tell herself that she would never do it again. Then the Enemy would slip his lies into her mind, and she would believe them and fall back into sin. She was back to where she started, trapped in a cycle, and utterly terrified that someday she would be married and still be addicted to porn. She would show up at church and hear her dad preaching on stage, saying, "Okay, men, if you have any kind of addiction to pornography, we have a group for you and a support system to get plugged into." Yet here she was, a girl, addicted to pornography with no help, with no support, and in complete isolation.

She felt broken and thought she was the only girl who struggled with this sin. Several times, she casually brought up the subject with other girls, but they made fun of the topic and shut it down. This led to a greater sense of isolation, loneliness, and feeling stuck. To combat these feelings, she would cover them up with her big personality and take on active roles like captaining the volleyball team and playing lead characters in the drama club. This helped compensate for the deep isolation she was experiencing inside. Then she would show up at youth group, sing on the worship team, and feel like she was able to compartmentalize her addiction.

But she felt like she was living two separate lives.

Maybe you have felt the same way, like there's a private "version" of you that is different from the public one. You may even wonder how you got to this point. After all, we never expect that we will someday live a "double life," but somehow we find ourselves following our own desires and believing the Enemy when he tells us that what we do in the dark is okay because no one will know. Eventually, we wake up and realize that the person we are when we are alone is completely different from who we are around others. And we become scared of letting people into our messiness.

But, my friend, the last thing the Lord wants for you is isolation. He wants you to invite Him, as well as other people, into your situation.

Stacia knew who Jesus was and she believed in Him, but she had put Him on the back burner. He wasn't number one in her life. She would see her dad preach on stage and think to herself,

I will never be able to do anything like him in ministry because of this huge stain on me. Although she desired to be a light for Christ in some way, the Enemy lied to her and told her that it would never be possible. So she discounted her desire to do ministry because she felt like she would not be allowed or qualified.

BRING THE BOX INTO THE LIGHT

As Stacia entered college and continued to struggle with porn, she began to beg the Lord to free her from this sin. While she confessed to Him what her heart was struggling with, Satan continued to tell her it was better that she didn't tell anyone about it. The Enemy made her terrified to share her secret. She knew that she didn't want to be stuck in this sin anymore but felt like her mind went into autopilot mode, and she continued to watch porn. With many kinds of addiction, our brains become wired in a certain way, so breaking the cycle and rewiring our brains takes a lot of time and effort. But Stacia became desperate and continued to pray to Jesus, asking Him to strengthen her and help her break free, to help her rewire her brain and control her thoughts. She started to set goals to wean herself off of watching porn. And slowly, she found herself watching less and less . . . and then none at all. There was never a marked moment of change that happened for her, but gradually she became free. She has now been free from pornography for more than nine years!

As I was interviewing her for this chapter, she kept telling me how she wished she had shared her struggle with others when she was going through it instead of waiting until she was free from it. She explained that after attending a small Christian college for two years, she felt the Lord calling her to transfer to a public four-year university. At this new university she found full and complete freedom. She started attending a small group in their campus ministry, and as she became more involved, she began to understand what Romans 8:1–2 truly meant. It says, "So now there is no condemnation for those who belong to Christ Jesus. And because you belong to him, the power of the life-giving Spirit has freed you from the power of sin that leads to death"(NLT). As this scripture sank in, she began to feel washed clean and was able to open up and share her story. Until this point, she had never told anyone what she had been walking through because the Enemy would say to her, *What you did was gross and disgusting, and you should be ashamed of yourself.*

But the Lord spoke to her and said, *Stacia, I want you to tell your story because it is going to show people My redemption and My love for them.* So, with tears running down her face, she finally verbalized to her small group at the public university this sin that had trapped her for so long. The reaction of the girls in the group surprised her—it was the complete opposite of what she had imagined. They all still loved her, accepted her, and saw her as a beloved child of God. As soon as she brought her secret out into the light, out of the box hidden in the dark, she felt a lightness from the Lord that she had never experienced before. It was true freedom. Her shame had been lifted off her shoulders. Not only that, she also wanted to tell more people about her freedom. She told her parents and other friends, and the Lord began to do what only He could do. He took her shame and used it to bring glory to His name.

Once people began to hear her story, she started getting invitations to speak at youth groups, conferences, and ministry events. Humbled and amazed at God's goodness, she gives her testimony frequently at churches, at youth groups, and on various podcasts, and she now leads a ministry where she mentors girls who struggle with pornography. Not only did the Lord free Stacia from her addiction, but He also gave her a platform to speak life and truth over women who struggle in similar ways. The Lord took what the Enemy meant for evil and instead used it to reveal His own goodness and glory.

However, this is not just a story of "look what God did for her," but it is an illustration of what He *can* also do for you! I don't want you to assume it was easy for her to break free. It wasn't. But even though it was one of the hardest things she's experienced, it happened. And it proves that healing is possible, not because of who we are but because of who God is.

> Healing is possible, not because of who we are
>
> but because of who God is.

Remember, Satan wants us to live in fear and darkness. He wants us to believe that the sin we are hiding is too shameful to tell others. He makes us afraid of what others might think if they only knew what we were struggling with. Because Satan knows that overcoming our battles is what leads us to freedom, he is going to do everything he can to stop us from sharing our stories. This is why Stacia kept saying during our interview, "Bringing other people into our shame is the most important thing we can do." She emphasized that she found freedom when she shared her struggle with others because she wasn't carrying it on her own anymore.

No matter what is bogging you down in shame, you aren't meant to carry it alone, my friend. Bring the box you are hiding into the light. You were meant to be a shining light for Christ in this world! He chose you, knowing the sin you would walk in. He chose you, knowing you are broken. He chose you, knowing every single thing about you, even before you were born. You are the perfect person for the job to shine His light in the most broken and darkest places. You know the places that I am talking about. You may even be there now. But nothing, absolutely nothing, can take away the fact that God loves you and calls you to be a light for Him. Your past does not disqualify you from being used by Him. With Him, and through Him, you are more than capable of shining His light.

Let's now look at a woman in the Bible whose résumé did not qualify her to be used by the Lord but who was chosen by God anyway.

THE LEAST LIKELY WOMAN

The story of Rahab is one of my absolute favorites. It shows the Lord's kindness in choosing the least likely people to do His greatest work. The story of Rahab takes place in Joshua 2. Joshua was trying to lead the Israelites into the Promised Land, so he sent two spies into Jericho to check it out first. Along the way, they came upon the house of a prostitute named Rahab and stayed there overnight. But the king of Jericho got word that two men from Israel had come to search out the land and had entered Rahab's house. The king sent orders to Rahab to bring the men out. She instead hid the two spies from the king's men and told them that they had already left her house. Once the king's men left, Rahab told the spies that she knew the Lord had given them the land, and that was why she didn't hand them over. Admitting her fear of Joshua's spies, she then asked if they would spare her and her family when they came back to overtake Jericho. The spies were grateful for her kindness and promised to repay her and do what she asked. They gave her a scarlet cord to put in her window to mark her home and save it from attack.

The book of Joshua continues with the story of how the Israelites finally made it to the Promised Land. The amazing way God orchestrated their journey is, without a doubt, a display of His power and sovereignty—everything from the spies' meeting with Rahab to the waters of the Jordan being parted to the thick fortress walls of Jericho falling down after the Israelites marched around them. But there is something key to recognize here: The Israelites would not have attempted to cross the Jordan and attack Jericho without knowing that the Lord's hand was in it. They knew this because Rahab told them that the Lord had given them the land. Rahab—a woman of bold faith who spent time listening to God—said He had given them the land, and she risked her life to protect the Israelite spies in order to do her part in God's mission.

Rahab, a prostitute, was the most unlikely hero in this story, yet God chose to use her. Think about that—a woman with a shameful past played a leading role in helping the Israelites into the Promised Land. Her past did not disqualify her from being used by the Lord. In fact, Rahab was more than qualified because of the One who was at work in and through her.

But what about us? It is easy for us to think, *God won't ever choose me to do that because I struggle with _____, or because I used to _____.* Those are the lies the Enemy tells us. Of course, the Enemy is going to do everything he can to keep us from doing good work for the kingdom and convince us that we are not qualified to be used by the Lord. But look at how the Lord used Rahab! I think that God intentionally used a woman with a shameful past to show us that when our faith is in Him, He can do the impossible. God wants us to see that in Him we are more than qualified—not because of our works but because of Jesus's work on the cross.

Recently in a Bible study I host for a group of ladies from my church, we studied the story of Rahab. At the end of the evening, I gave everyone a piece of paper and had them write down the things they felt disqualified them from being used by the Lord. After they finished writing, I had them walk over to the fireplace in my living room and throw the piece of paper into the fire. We watched as each paper turned into ash and dust. Dust is beautiful because it is the substance that God used to make man in Genesis 2:7: "Then the LORD God formed a man from the dust of the ground and breathed into his nostrils the breath of life, and the man became a living being." He literally made us from dust! And not only that, but we see in Isaiah 61:3 that God gives us "beauty for ashes" (NLT). He can make anything from anything to bring glory to His name. God takes what seems worthless and dirty and makes beauty out of it. God can take your past and bring meaning to it as well.

> Rahab was more than qualified because of the
> One who was at work in and through her.

You've probably heard a speaker or pastor say, "God doesn't call the qualified, He qualifies the called." My friend, nothing disqualifies you from being used by the Lord. In Him, and because of Him, you are qualified. You might be surprised where He wants to use you. Just as you saw in the story of Rahab, God uses the least likely people to do His best work. So throw your

past and your list of disqualifications into the fire and watch for
the beauty that He can make from the ashes.

RUN THE RACE

Jesus knew shame. He was nailed to a cross, the most shameful
way to die at that time, and stripped of all His clothing. Yet He
defeated shame on the cross through what should have been the
most humiliating death. And what did God do? He brought
glory to His name by giving the world the greatest gift of redemption through Jesus's death and resurrection. I love that the
Lord paints a picture for us of bearing our shame and still bringing glory to God's name through Jesus's example. We no longer
have to live trapped in our sin and our shame, because it was
nailed to the cross. Hebrews 12:1–3 says,

> Therefore, since we are surrounded by such a great cloud of
> witnesses, let us throw off everything that hinders and the sin
> that so easily entangles. And let us run with perseverance the
> race marked out for us, fixing our eyes on Jesus, the pioneer
> and perfecter of faith. For the joy set before him he endured
> the cross, scorning its shame, and sat down at the right hand
> of the throne of God. Consider him who endured such op-
> position from sinners, so that you will not grow weary and lose
> heart.

There is a race set before you. There is a story written for your
life. You were created for a specific purpose, but the Enemy wants
to do everything he can to make you believe that there is no reason for your life. In these verses in Hebrews, we are told to throw
off the weight and any sin that entangles us! In other words, get
the weight of your sin off your shoulders by confessing it and

giving it to the Lord, and bring others into it as well. Once you've confessed, you will be able to run the race that the Lord has set before you without feeling like you aren't capable or worthy to do so. As Jesus endured the cross, He knew the joy that was right around the corner. And my friend, that same joy is accessible to us! We may feel like our sin weighs us down or the darkness of the world is too overwhelming, but God's greatest promise is that at the end of our race, we get to be with Him in heaven.

When I think of a race, my mind goes first to swimming. I grew up swimming competitively, and before a big race I would shave my legs and my arms and put on the tightest swimsuit and the best cap and goggles. It was uncomfortable to wear a tight swimsuit and annoying to shave my arms, but in order to swim my best and fastest, I made sure there was nothing on me that would hinder my race. As soon as I dove into the pool, I would immediately search for the black tile that lined the bottom of the pool. Keeping my head in perfect alignment and fixing my eyes on the line below were key to swimming my best race.

> As Jesus endured the cross, He knew the joy
> that was right around the corner.

I love how this analogy ties into the verses in Hebrews above. Throw off anything that entangles you and put all your effort into the race set before you with your eyes fixed on that straight line— Jesus. Run this race of life with everything you've got.

So, why don't we do everything we can to run this race here on earth to the best of our ability? Why not push through the things that are hard and heavy and fight the good fight of faith to be a bright and shining light for Christ? It is 100 percent possible. It may not be the easiest thing we will do, but life with Jesus isn't meant to be easy. It is designed to help us depend on Him for strength—not live from our own strength. This world tells us that once we have a comfortable life, then we have it all. But if we are striving to live a life like Jesus, it's not likely to be comfortable.

Just like Stacia and Rahab, you are also called by God to live out His purpose for you. A big question to ask yourself is, "Would I rather live an uncomfortable life fulfilling my call, or a comfortable life that is unfulfilling and that ignores the God-given call placed on me?" I don't know about you, but when it comes to my final breath, I want to be known for being a sparkling light for Christ. If this resonates with you, I want you to know that I believe in you and I am right there with you!

Let's start today. Today is a great day to open up and let others in. Today is a great day to throw off sin. Today is a great day to fix your eyes on Jesus. Today is a great day to run the race set before you. Today is a great day to walk in your identity as a child of the Light.

Maybe you are thinking, *Okay, but how?* I promise we will get there in a few chapters. Keep pushing through and holding on. We are in this race together.

ARISE AND SHINE

- Open up to someone about what you have kept hidden in a box in your life.
- Write on a piece of paper what you feel disqualifies you from being used by the Lord. Then throw it in a fire or cut it up into a bunch of little pieces. Journal about that experience.
- Pray and ask the Lord to strengthen you to run the race that is set before you.

4

SHATTERED PIECES

Reflecting the Light of Christ
Through Our Brokenness

EARLY ONE SUNNY SPRING morning, I went downstairs from my bedroom into our kitchen to make myself some coffee. As I put the grounds in our espresso machine and waited for my milk to froth, I felt defeated. The night before, my husband and I had been lying in bed and I had one of those moments where I should have held my tongue but instead decided to bring up everything he had been doing that bothered me. (If you are engaged or newly married or have even been married forty years, I highly recommend you *do not* do this).

I knew I had hurt his feelings because the tone of his voice completely changed. I was instantly convicted of what I had done and realized I needed to apologize. After I said I was sorry, we both rolled over and tried to go to sleep. I tossed and turned for hours, replaying what I said over and over, making myself more upset at what I had done. What I said to him was not out of a kind and loving heart but rather came from the stress and bitterness I had been feeling from work, relationships, and the devastating situations I kept seeing on the news. It took me forever to fall asleep because I felt like the worst wife in the world.

As I waited for my coffee to brew, terrible thoughts played over and over in my mind. *How could someone love me when I just pointed out everything that was selfishly bothering me? How do I deserve to be loved by this selfless man? I don't deserve forgiveness. I feel like a fake in every area in my life.* What started as good conviction turned into a big spiral of lies. I know now they were thoughts from the Enemy and completely not true. But they *felt* so real to me at the time. They ate at me and made me feel like my brokenness was just plain ugly. I felt shame. If only I could take back everything I had said and everything I had made my husband feel. I kept wishing that I could just be a better wife.

Finally, my coffee was ready. I poured the frothed milk over my iced espresso and prepared to spend some time with Jesus. As I was walking from our kitchen into the living room, I noticed a blue image that was reflected onto the wall behind our front door. As I stared at it, I realized that the rising sun was shining through the blue stained-glass window. The window I always complained about.

You see, when my husband and I moved into our house, one of the things I really disliked about it was that it had random stained-glass windows. They are not the beautiful modern stained-glass windows. No, these have pink roses on them that make you feel like you are in the movie *Beauty and the Beast.* Our front door even has a little blue stained-glass window. It made no sense to me and was something I couldn't wait to replace. In fact, when people came over to the house I would say, "Don't worry, we'll eventually be getting rid of these windows."

But this particular morning, I saw something I had never noticed before. Cast on the wall was a perfect image of the door's stained-glass window. You could see in detail every broken piece that had been used to make it a true work of art. For the first time, I saw its beauty. And it brought me joy.

As I went to the living room to read my Bible, the Lord interrupted my thoughts. It was as if He said, *Allyson, you are just like that window. You are often broken and shattered—too broken to put yourself back together. And yet there is beauty in your broken pieces, and I see the masterpiece that you are.* It was a beautiful revelation; I visualized the Lord taking each of my broken pieces and putting them together, binding them with His love and grace. Just like in a stained-glass window, each broken piece is hand placed into a very specific spot by the Artist Himself. He makes a beautiful masterpiece out of what we thought was a disaster.

The shame I had been feeling was from the Enemy and not from the Lord. While what I did was sinful, and I needed to recognize it and repent, the Lord's conviction isn't meant to lead us into feeling shame. Conviction is the Lord calling us higher. As my mother-in-law says, "Conviction is always for our good and God's glory. Shame is from Satan for our defeat and to silence us, making us feel paralyzed."

I was initially experiencing conviction over the words I had said, knowing what I said was wrong and unkind. But then the Enemy had taken hold of my thoughts, and I spiraled into feeling as if my very being was wrong. Satan loves to use this tactic on all of us. Remember, conviction is good when it leads to confession because that confession brings freedom and a sense of closeness to the Lord. But the Enemy doesn't like it when we want to be closer to Jesus, so he sneaks in and makes us believe that we don't deserve nearness to Jesus. The sense of being separated from the Lord causes us to spiral downward toward shame amid a bunch of lies.

Now that I am able to appreciate the beauty of my stained-glass window, I like to believe that each tragedy, hardship, and instance of pain that happens in our lives is like a skillfully shaped, broken piece of glass. As we live our lives and experience heart-shattering incidents, we generate and collect more broken pieces of glass, and the Creator forms beautiful artwork by masterfully joining our fragments together. God takes each broken piece and places it precisely where it needs to be, creating something beautiful and breathtaking. All the while, His Light is shining through these broken pieces, bringing light into the darkness. The resulting work of art reflects the beautiful story of what we have seen, felt, and experienced.

BROKEN GLASS CAN BE SHARP AND PAINFUL

Let's take a moment here to recognize the very hard and painful things that you have walked through in your life. Have you had experiences that you feel can never be redeemed or used for good? Do you feel as if there are things in your life that keep you from fully living in your identity as a child of God? If so, I want to remind you that our God is a redeemer. He takes what the Enemy meant for evil and turns it into something good.[1] He is not a God who inflicts pain, but rather He takes the pain that we have experienced in this fallen and dark world and shines His light into it. He is a God who is in the business of redemption, of creating beauty, not of shaming and belittling.

God takes our shattered pieces and creates a marvelous mosaic. I love to picture Jesus gathering all the broken pieces of glass that represent me. I imagine Him looking at a bunch of fragments on a table, almost like a puzzle before it is put together. He grasps each piece so gently with His loving and careful hands. He speaks life and purpose over each piece. Then He starts creating the masterpiece. He picks up the shiny pink oval representing the patient who almost took his life. He then chooses the periwinkle triangle that denotes the anger and bitterness of my heart and places it next to the oval. He takes the piece that has sparkling gold specks in it, representing the heartache of a broken friendship, and places it among the others.

God takes our shattered pieces and

creates a marvelous mosaic.

He picks up your emerald-green hexagon, the one that represents your strained relationship with your mom, and places it next to the cherry-red square that symbolizes the abuse you experienced as a child. He grabs the oblong piece that looks like sea glass, representing the hurt you have experienced in your marriage, and sets it next to the rectangular shard that signifies the mental health issues you are experiencing. He takes the sparkling silver moon shape that represents the fear that fills your heart and sets it next to the worn and smooth light blue piece that stands for the loneliness you feel.

He does this with every single shattered part of who we are. He holds each fragile piece with tenderness and loving care. God wants us to see the beautiful masterpiece that He sees in each of us. He wants us to see how everything we experience becomes part of who we are.

God doesn't stop with the arrangement of our pieces. He then shines His light through us, creating a reflection of His masterpiece through our once-broken fragments, now made whole in Him. And notice this: *It isn't the stained glass itself shining but rather the Light shining through it.*

How different God's view is from that of Satan—who loves to showcase only the individual shattered pieces. I know it is so easy to fixate on the one destructive moment, the mistake we made, or the horrible thing we witnessed. But remember, that one piece doesn't define us. When it is placed among all the other fragments, it finds its home. It is washed with the grace of the Father. It has a place in the masterpiece of who you are.

In my home that morning, I realized the window and the sun had to be aligned before the stained-glass image clearly projected onto the wall. Similarly, when we are in alignment with the Lord, His light shines brightly through us and we most clearly reflect who He is. I was also reminded that the light of the Lord never stops shining, just as the sun never stops shining, even if we can't always see it.

RESISTING THE WORLD'S PULL

I realize we live in a culture where many think being in alignment with the Lord is probably the least appealing thing to strive for. Voices from all different directions are screaming for our attention. There is an ever-present Enemy who wants to pull us away from the Lord, so he does everything he can to get us to focus on other things—even things that may *seem* to be good for us but in fact pull us out of alignment with Christ. We must also remember that on this side of heaven we will never be a perfect representation of the Lord. It's impossible for us to reflect the exact image of God because of our sinful nature, but we can strive to do our best to reflect as much of Him as we can.

If we are doing things that draw us away from who God is and how He calls us to live, we project a negative and inaccurate image of Him. Some influences are easy to evaluate as right or wrong, good or evil. But a big gray area can exist around certain choices that might *seem* good but ultimately are not, especially when we reason that "everyone else is doing it" or "it will make me happy."

For example, so much of our culture tries to convince us it is cool to sleep with multiple people, get drunk every weekend, do all the drugs that make you feel good, make yourself famous, do five jobs at a time to make a bunch of money, lie to get yourself where you want to be, watch people having sex, or speak in a way that tears people down if it makes you feel good. The underlying theme says, "In all that you do, life is all about you and your happiness." These actions are not worse than any other sin, but because they have become commonplace in today's culture they often get interpreted as acceptable by worldly standards.

Sadly, everywhere I go I see people living life solely focused on their own happiness, searching for it in things of the world. Maybe they don't know—or maybe they have chosen not to believe—that we are supposed to be living *not* of this world. This means that what others are doing might be the very activities we should reject.

> "I do not ask that you take them out of the world,
>
> but that you keep them from the evil one."

The phrase "not of this world" comes from John 17:14 when Jesus says, "I have given them your word, and the world has hated them because they are not of the world, just as I am not of the world" (ESV). If this is your first time reading this verse, it actually comes from a prayer that Jesus prayed right before He was betrayed and arrested. The fact that Jesus specifically prayed for you and me is so encouraging and beautiful. He doesn't only say the words above but continues on in verses 15–18:

I do not ask that you take them out of the world, but that you keep them from the evil one. They are not of the world, just as I am not of the world. Sanctify them in the truth; your word is truth. As you sent me into the world, so I have sent them into the world. (ESV)

So, just as Jesus was not of the world, we are to live not of the world. But trust me, I get it, it is *hard* to withstand temptation. I am fully guilty of giving into it at times, rationalizing that maybe *this thing* or *that action* isn't all that bad, right? The Enemy does a really great job of convincing us certain things are okay: *Everyone else does it*, or *This is just temporary*, or *Happiness is what I need to focus on*.

Yet, it's in Christ that we are made new.[2] And although it is hard, my friend, there is so much hope! By His power our minds can be renewed. We weren't made to live a life where we chase moments that will give us only temporary spurts of happiness. And please hear me: I am not saying that happiness isn't from the Lord. Rather we must be careful with what we chase and why we chase it. We are called to live a life chasing the One who can give us everlasting joy! If your heart's desire is to reflect Christ, ask the Holy Spirit to illuminate your mind to the things you may be doing of darkness that are affecting your representation of Him. Remember, conviction is not shame. The Lord sees every single thing we do, and His desire is for us to live a life that points to the goodness of who He is! He wants to help you and redeem you, not scorn you and make you feel like you have no hope.

The Bible calls us to be children of the Light:

For you were once darkness, but now you are light in the Lord.
Live as children of light (for the fruit of the light consists in all
goodness, righteousness and truth) and find out what pleases
the Lord. Have nothing to do with the fruitless deeds of darkness, but rather expose them. (Ephesians 5:8–11)

Living as a child of light is living in the goodness, righteousness, and truth of the Lord. As the verse says, the deeds of darkness are fruitless. They don't add to our lives, and they don't point
to Jesus.

We also see in the book of Isaiah that the people were looking
for light but felt they could find only darkness.[3] Isaiah 59:9 says,
"So there is no justice among us, and we know nothing about
right living. We look for light but find only darkness. We look for
bright skies but walk in gloom" (NLT). They had been living in sin
for so long and doing what they thought was best for themselves.
They had given themselves over to darkness by choosing to walk
in ways that were against what the Lord had called them to.[4] But
then Isaiah calls them higher into truth. He says,

Arise, Jerusalem! Let your light shine for all to see.
  For the glory of the LORD rises to shine on you.
Darkness as black as night covers all the nations of the earth,
  but the glory of the LORD rises and appears over you.
  (Isaiah 60:1–2, NLT)

The people of Jerusalem were feeling trapped in the darkness
of the world around them as well as in their own sin. And then
Isaiah tells them to arise and shine because the glory of the Lord
is shining on them. Isaiah calls them higher. Isaiah calls them
into the truth.

We, too, are called higher. The heart of this book is to help you see the true potential you have in Jesus because of Jesus. You are not trapped in darkness. It is better for us than even those we read about in the book of Isaiah because we now have the hope of Jesus! The actual Light of this world came down and lived a human life, and then He gave His life for us. He deserves everything we have because everything we have is from Him! The darkness of this world can feel overwhelming, yes. The darkness we sometimes partake in seems appealing, yes. You may feel inadequate to shine the light of Christ, yes. But that is where the Enemy wants us to stay! That is the darkness those in the book of Isaiah were feeling completely trapped in. But then we see Isaiah tell the people to arise and shine!

My friend, I am saying to you right now, "[Insert your name here], arise! Let your light shine for all to see. For the glory of the Lord rises to shine on you."

ACKNOWLEDGING THE CHALLENGE

As I was writing this chapter, I almost deleted the first part of the section you just read. To be honest, I was afraid to say things that may cause you to feel shame for what you have done in the past or what you may do in the future. But I chose to keep the section because I know deep down inside your heart you want to live a life full of light. So right now, I pray over you against any lies of the Enemy that would cause you to feel shame. Conviction can scare us because the feeling that we've done something wrong can make us uncomfortable. But we cannot base everything we do and believe off our feelings. Yes, our feelings are important, and we need to listen to them. They can't always be our ultimate guide. Our ultimate guide is the Word of God.

It is fully possible to change your ways. It is fully possible to renew your mind. It is fully possible to find joy in the things that may not seem popular to the world. You are capable. You aren't stuck. The potential you have is endless in Jesus. Lean on Him. Ask for His strength to help you say no to the dark things in your life. He wants to help you. He hears your prayers and your pleas. You weren't made to stay in the dark; you were made to be a child of light. You were made to be a walking reflection of Jesus. What a beautiful gift!

I want to remind you that nothing can take away the fact that we are made in God's image. The Bible tells us that in the beginning God created all of mankind in His image.[5] That is and always will be our identity. John Piper says, "God created us for this: to live our lives in a way that makes him look more like the greatness and the beauty and the infinite worth that he really is. . . . This is what it means to be created in the image of God."[6] You are an image bearer of the Most High King—what an honor and a privilege that is! Let's not shrink back from that identity because of the lies of the Enemy, but rather let's stand strong in the truth that we are walking reflections of Christ!

What binds our broken pieces together is the beautiful grace and redemption of the Lord.

As I look again at my stained-glass window, I am reminded of one important detail: *What binds our broken pieces together is the beautiful grace and redemption of the Lord.* He sees our pain. He sees what we have been through. He sees what we struggle with, and yet His grace is so kind and unending. We are imperfect people, and on this earth we will always struggle with sin. But when Jesus died on the cross for us, all sin was forgiven and washed away. It was the greatest act of love ever to be done. Jesus, the one deserving of all glory, took the punishment for us who aren't even deserving. Out of His great and deep love for us He chose to carry all our sin on that cross.

When we say yes to Jesus, His grace infiltrates every single area of our lives. And the grace of the Lord is something we are not to take advantage of. We are not to think, *I can do this immoral thing because God has already forgiven me.* Doing so is putting our desires in the center of our lives rather than chasing after who the Lord calls us to be. To be clear, I am not suggesting this is what you are doing; rather, I just want to remind you to put the desires of your flesh away.

My friend, although living a life that reflects Jesus is hard, it will be the most fulfilling choice you ever make. Following Jesus isn't easy, living a life going against the grain of this world isn't easy, but hard things have great reward. And in following Jesus we get the greatest reward: eternal life with the Father. An eternal life free of pain, brokenness, hurt, sickness, and darkness. An earthly life chasing after light leads to an eternal life with the Light forever.

—◆—

Because you might have found this chapter heavy, let's take a pause to pray:

Lord, I want to thank You for Your unending grace. Help me to see what You are trying to speak to me right now. I want to incline my ear to hear from You. I want to seek after Your heart. If there is any area in my life that I need to lay at Your feet today, I ask that You reveal it to me. I also ask that any lie of the Enemy stays far away from me, in Jesus's name. I ask for forgiveness for

the ways I have sinned against You. I thank and praise You for
being my redeemer. Thank You for forgiving me, seeing me for who
I am, and loving me all the same. Help me be a light for You.
Align my heart with Yours. Instill within me the desire to be the
best reflection of You that I can be. Take away anything in my life
that hinders my representation of You. Amen.

ARISE AND SHINE

- Read Isaiah 60.
- Journal any feelings or thoughts this chapter brought up for you. Lay it all at the feet of Jesus. Then ask Him what He wants to speak to you over what you wrote.
- On a sticky note, write "Arise and Shine" and place it on your bathroom mirror.

PART II

ILLUMINATING LIGHT

It started when God said, "Light up the darkness!" and our lives filled up with light as we saw and understood God in the face of Christ, all bright and beautiful.

—2 Corinthians 4:6, msg

5

TRANSFORMING TRUTH

Renewing Our Minds with God's Word

WHEN I SAT DOWN to write this chapter, I told my husband I didn't feel in the mood to write. I said, "I'm just not a good enough writer, I'm not qualified enough, and I feel like I don't know what to say." I was struggling with motivation because these negative thoughts were affecting me. The fact that I was insecure about my writing at this particular point is pure irony because *this is the chapter where we are going to dive into the power of declaring truth over our lives when our thoughts are fixated on all the negative and dark things happening around us!*

My husband kindly reminded me that I was living my dream getting to do this, but I was still questioning my worth and calling. He told me that if I kept speaking those lies over myself, it would continue to be hard to write. But if I chose to speak life and God's truth over myself, that would empower me to do what I am called to do. Friend, my husband is right. Replacing lies with truth is remarkably powerful and can completely change our lives.

I did what my husband told me to do. I declared the truth of
Jesus over myself rather than sit in the weight of the lies of the
Enemy. What a good reminder that I need this message too. I
also realize that changing my thought patterns is something that
will be a lifelong learning process.

NONSTOP THOUGHTS

I recently read an article that says a human has more than six
thousand thoughts per day while awake.[1] Researchers were able
to detect when a thought began and when it ended and found
that some thoughts can last quite a while and others can come
and go in a short amount of time. So, if we are awake for sixteen
hours per day, that averages to at least six thoughts per minute,
most likely a lot more.

Take a moment to consider how many of your thoughts you
try to actively control. Probably not that many. Most of us have
an initial thought and then our mind goes on a long rabbit trail
and we end up thinking about something completely different.
Sometimes our thoughts end up spiraling and creating false re-
alities in our minds, making us feel alone, unwanted, forgotten,
and so many other negative things—all because our minds wan-
dered and focused on thoughts that aren't even true.

I have learned that our mind is one of the main places where
the Enemy attacks us. Since the beginning of time, Satan has
been placing doubts and lies in our minds, causing us to act in
ways we shouldn't or think in ways that tear us and others down.
It's pretty sneaky and clever. As we see in Genesis 3, Satan places
doubt in Eve's mind: "Did God really say, 'You must not eat from
any tree in the garden'?"[2] Eve disobeyed after Satan's lie caused
her to doubt what God told her. It makes me think of all the
times Satan has placed that exact thought in my head, *Did God*

really say _____? and then I respond according to what I *thought* to be true or what the Enemy made me believe to be true.

The Enemy tries to control our thoughts because they lead to our feelings and actions. As Jennie Allen says in *Get Out of Your Head:*

> What we believe and what we think about matters, and the enemy knows it. And he is determined to get in your head to distract you from doing good and to sink you so deep that you feel helpless, overwhelmed, shut down, and incapable of rising to make a difference for the kingdom of God.[3]

The Enemy knows that our thoughts control what we do, so of course he is going to attack us in that area to try to control us.

So, how do we stop the Enemy from attacking our minds? Well, entire books have been written on just this topic. (I've given you some book recommendations at the end of this chapter.) Together we are going to look at the one way the Bible tells us to fight the lies: by knowing and using the weapon of God's Truth.

To be a light in this dark world, we must be rooted in the Light of life.

In his transformative book *Winning the War in Your Mind,* Craig Groeschel says, "If Satan's primary weapon is lies, then our greatest counter-weapon is the truth of God's Word. Not just reading the Bible but learning to wield Scripture as a divine weapon. God wants us to view his Word that way."[4] The Bible is very clear about the power that God's Word has. Hebrews 4:12

says, "For the word of God is alive and active. Sharper than any double-edged sword, it penetrates even to dividing soul and spirit, joints and marrow; it judges the thoughts and attitudes of the heart." The Bible also tells us to put on the full armor of God, including His Word:

> Finally, be strong in the Lord and in his mighty power. Put on the full armor of God, so that you can take your stand against the devil's schemes. For our struggle is not against flesh and blood, but against the rulers, against the authorities, against the powers of this dark world and against the spiritual forces of evil in the heavenly realms. Therefore put on the full armor of God, so that when the day of evil comes, you may be able to stand your ground, and after you have done everything, to stand. Stand firm then, with the belt of truth buckled around your waist, with the breastplate of righteousness in place, and with your feet fitted with the readiness that comes from the gospel of peace. In addition to all this, take up the shield of faith, with which you can extinguish all the flaming arrows of the evil one. Take the helmet of salvation and the sword of the Spirit, which is the word of God. (Ephesians 6:10–17)

In this description of the armor of God, His Word is mentioned twice, once as a weapon and second as a defensive piece. Not only are we to have the sword of the Spirit, which is His Word, but we are also to have the belt of truth. We must be grounded in God's Word and know with all of our hearts what His Truth says in order to combat the devil's schemes. We must speak the truth, the Word, to shut down those lies.

To be a light in this dark world, we must be rooted in the Light of life and have God's Word written on our hearts. The more we know the truth of the One who is the Light of the world, the more equipped we will be to stand against the tactics of the Enemy. I like to picture the sword of the Spirit like a lightsaber that instantly destroys any darkness it encounters. That is how powerful the Word of God is—strong enough to knock down any lies of the Enemy that may have a hold on us.

DECLARING TRUTH OVER OURSELVES

My friend Darsha discovered the power of declaring truth over herself, and it completely changed her life. Growing up, she wasn't a Christian. In middle school, she believed that hating people was cool and that being cynical made her feel good. She began to believe that disliking people was her identity. Darsha didn't know it then, but the Enemy had a hold on her thoughts.

Darsha was invited to a Young Life event at the age of sixteen and met the girl who would become her Young Life leader. At this time in Darsha's life, she was still stuck in the belief that being cynical toward people, especially new people, was how she should live. This Young Life leader pursued Darsha even though she did not want to be pursued. Her leader loved her, asked her questions, and showed compassion toward her. She made Darsha feel seen and known, and deep down in Darsha's heart that was exactly what she was longing for. This leader's love led to Darsha encountering and coming to know Jesus. She then came to realize that Jesus was the least cynical person.

Darsha's eyes were opened to the fact that Jesus loved every single person, along with all that they carried. She once heard a friend say, "How could I be against someone who Jesus is for?" From hearing this, she had a revelation that even the people whom she least liked and those who she thought were really annoying were Jesus's favorites. The Lord vividly spoke to her, *Every human is My favorite person.* Darsha felt the Lord convict her to love people better. With this insight, she discovered that when she said she didn't like people, she was covering up her own uncomfortable feelings of shyness. Other people told her, "You're so shy. You're so quiet." And she began to believe it for herself. Darsha thought, *I'm too nervous to talk, and so I must not want to talk to people,* when actually, she did want to talk to them.

For so long, Darsha saw her identity as shy and cynical. How could she change? She began to realize that everything she spoke over herself was a declaration—both good and bad. Even things like "I don't know what to say" or "I can never change." So Darsha started speaking only affirming words over herself: "I can change. I am not shy. I have important things to say." It was that simple. She would both think these things in her mind and say them out loud.

As she began to speak against the lies that she had heard as she grew up, she started to walk confidently. She realized she was not a shy person but rather she had words to say that deeply mattered.

Truly, now she is one of the most outgoing people I know. Her voice is powerful. Her words have greatly impacted my life. The Lord has done a mighty work within her and is using her to impact people in ways she could never have imagined. All because she chose to declare the truth of the Lord over herself. She chose to speak the identity God declared over her life rather than the identity the world spoke over her. For the past ten years, she has been living in the fruit of those declarations she repeated.

When interviewing Darsha for this chapter, I asked her how she took that first step to start declaring truth over her life. After all, it's one thing to say you want to start declaring truth and another to actually do it and stick with it until transformation happens. She explained that any time she starts to get nervous or believe the lies the Enemy sneaks in, it has become like muscle memory to replace that thought with a declaration of truth. Replacing her thoughts all started when she recognized the need to interrupt her thoughts. She realized that with God's help, she had the power to replace the thoughts that were tearing her down with truth that would build her up.

Jennie Allen's book *Get Out of Your Head* focuses on the fact that this one interrupting thought can completely change our thought patterns: "I have a choice." Jennie says,

> If you have trusted in Jesus as your Savior, you have the power of God in you to choose! You are no longer a slave to passions, to lusts, to strongholds, to sin of any kind. You have a God-given, God-empowered, God-redeemed ability to choose what you think about. You have a choice regarding where you focus your energy. You have a choice regarding what you live for.[5]

We have the power to change our thought patterns. We have the power to choose to declare over ourselves the one thing that can completely change our lives: God's Word. It simply begins as a choice. A split-second choice! Darsha shared with me that it isn't just a one-time choice that will change us. We must choose to declare the truth over and over again. Repetitively declaring God's Word over ourselves will end up transforming us into believing in who He has created us to be.

With the strength of the Lord we can fight

against the lies of the Enemy.

But it isn't our own power that can enable our minds to change and be renewed, it's the power of the Holy Spirit. In fact, in the Bible, we are told multiple times that by the power of the Holy Spirit our minds and thought patterns can be renewed. For example:

> Since you have heard about Jesus and have learned the truth that comes from him, throw off your old sinful nature and your former way of life, which is corrupted by lust and deception. Instead, let the Spirit renew your thoughts and attitudes. (Ephesians 4:21–23, NLT)

> Don't copy the behavior and customs of this world, but let God transform you into a new person by changing the way you think. Then you will learn to know God's will for you, which is good and pleasing and perfect. (Romans 12:2, NLT)

> Put on your new nature, and be renewed as you learn to know your Creator and become like him. (Colossians 3:10, NLT)

Friend, it is 100 percent possible for your mind to be renewed. It is possible for you to change the way you think and get out of what feels like a constant spiral. It's probably not going to happen in the blink of an eye (although I do fully believe God is capable of doing that). But rather, renewing our minds is a lifelong process we will go through with the Lord. It's recognizing our need for a Savior. It's knowing that on our own we cannot do it, but with the strength of the Lord we can fight against the lies of the Enemy.

I get it; it's a lot easier said than done. But don't worry. I won't leave you hanging! Let's dive into some practical ways we can incorporate this truth into our lives to help us begin the renewal process.

APPLYING TRUTH TO OUR LIVES

We've been talking about the power of declaring truth over the lies that we can easily believe, so let's look at ways to actually do that. I want to share with you four practical steps that have impacted me and those around me when it comes to learning to declare God's Word over our lives.

The first way is to **speak the truth out loud.** I have listed some declarations you can say over yourself. Circle the ones that resonate with you the most. You can use them in the next exercise as well. So get yourself comfortable, grab a pen, and speak these declarations out loud over yourself!

I am a beloved child of God.
I am chosen.
I am redeemed.
I am a child of Light.
I can do what God has called me to do in His strength.
No darkness can ever overcome the light of Christ.
My past does not define who I am in Christ.
God can use me for His glory.
I am a light for Christ.
I am fully known.
I have purpose.
I am beautiful the way God made me.
I have everything that I need.
The Lord provides for me.
I am a friend of God.

I am accepted.

I am renewed.

I am never alone.

I am God's handiwork.

I am protected.

I am set free.

The light of Christ is within me!

I challenge you to say these declarations over yourself every time you pick this book up and read it. Mark these pages—fold over the corners or put a sticky note on them. Do whatever will help you come back and declare these truths until they seep deep into your heart. These aren't made-up manifestations but rather are statements of the active truth and Word of God. You can choose to say them out loud even if they are hard for you to believe right now. But that is the whole point. The Enemy wants us to feel far from believing these truths, when in fact they are the truest statements that exist! Just keep repeating them. Make it a habit. Slowly incorporate the practice of speaking these declarations over yourself into your daily routine.

The second activity you can do to help remember these truths is to **write them down and put them in places you see often.** Ask yourself what declaration of truth you need to be reminded of most. Write it on a sticky note and put it on your bathroom mirror, fridge, doorways, car steering wheel, or any other spot you see frequently throughout the day. Make a phone background of it or put a reminder in your phone that will pop up on your screen daily. The more we read the truth, the more likely we are to remember it and memorize it and use it to counteract the lies of the Enemy.

The third activity you can do (which is one of my personal favorites) is **write down in a journal all the things you are think-**

ing and feeling. Write a letter to God telling Him where you feel like you are. Don't hold any feelings or thoughts back. Your deepest and most intense thoughts don't scare the Lord, and He wants to hear them from you. Once you've written it, ask the Lord what He wants to speak to you about what you told Him. Listen for what truth He wants to tell you. Ask Him to show you where He is amid all that you are feeling and thinking. What constant biblical truth does He want to replace your wavering thoughts with? Any thought that is from the Lord is gentle, kind, and for your good. He wants to speak to you. Write down what He says. Remember, draw near to Him, and He will draw near to you.[6]

A fourth way to help us interrupt our negative thoughts is to **share our thoughts with others.** How often do you share the thoughts that keep you awake at night with someone else? Do you let people in on what is tearing you apart or making you feel less than? I'm guessing the answer is probably *not very often* or maybe *not at all.* (If you do open up to people often, that's a good thing!) But friend, there is so much power in bringing to light the thoughts we hide in the dark.

Something I have been doing lately is telling my husband the thoughts I have when they are attacking my mind, just like the insecurity I mentioned at the beginning of this chapter. For example, I have been struggling with my body image recently. That isn't something I have struggled with a lot in the past. But lately, it has been really hard. The Enemy has been placing these lies in my mind about what I look like. The other night I told my husband, "Babe, I feel like I have gained so much weight. I feel like my body is so ugly right now, and I keep feeling like I don't love my body." He was able to remind me that my body, just as it is, was made by God and for God. This body is loved, this body has a purpose, and this body was made to do what only this body can.

He helped me interrupt the lies I was believing with the truth. That would not have happened if I had kept my thoughts and feelings to myself. Who knows where the thoughts would have continued to go if I had kept them inside where the Enemy could continue to attack?

Saying out loud what we are struggling with takes the power away from the Enemy. When we keep things to ourselves, he can attack and attack and attack. But when we let someone in on what we are thinking, it gives that thought less power and allows space for that person to help us see the truth instead of the lie.

> **Saying out loud what we are struggling with takes the power away from the Enemy.**

Who can you confide in when you are struggling with the lies of the Enemy? I want to challenge you to find a point person—whether it be a spouse, significant other, mom or dad, friend, or pastor—you can turn to. It doesn't make you any less of a person. It doesn't reflect negatively on your character. In fact, when we let people in, it shows boldness and humility. Letting others in to help us with our thoughts is not a sign of weakness but instead is a sign of strength.

Think about it: Wouldn't you want a friend to share their thoughts with you when they are struggling so you can help them see the truth of who they are in the Lord? For me, the answer to that question is 100 percent yes. I want to help my friends see who the Lord says they are! Imagine a world where we all help one another recognize the lies of the Enemy and then speak truth over one another to replace those lies. Let's be people like that. Let's be friends like that. Let's allow our friends to be that for us.

The combination of these four exercises has greatly helped me rewire my brain away from the lies I so easily had believed. It's taken time though. Learning to retrain the way we think is a lifelong learning process. But it is so very important. Jesus says in John 8:31–32 (ESV), "If you abide in my word, you are truly my disciples, and you will know the truth, and the truth will set you free." God's truth will set us free. Not only free from sin but also free from the bondage of the Enemy's lies.

My friend, you are called to be a light for Christ. Whatever lie the Enemy is trying to speak over you has no hold on you, in Jesus's name.

You are a light for Christ.

You are a light for Christ.

You are a light for Christ.

ARISE AND SHINE

- Who can you speak truth over today? Send them a text.
- Come up with two of your own declarations of truth in response to the frequent lies of the Enemy you believe.
- Reach out to a friend this week and let them in on the thoughts you have been struggling with.
- For further reading, check out any of these: *Winning the War in Your Mind* by Craig Groeschel, *Get Out of Your Head* by Jennie Allen, *Live No Lies* by John Mark Comer, or *Switch On Your Brain* by Dr. Caroline Leaf.

CLOSER TO THE LIGHT

How to Draw Near to God When It Feels Dark

EVERYONE WHO WORKS NIGHT shifts tolerates them differently. Some people adapt easily, whereas others struggle a lot. Unfortunately, I fall into that second camp.

Night shifts are just a part of being a nurse, especially when you are brand-new. I had been working the night shift for about two years when the lack of sleep began to really take a toll on my body. Not sleeping well between shifts added to the stress of my job. Not only did it affect me at work, but it also affected my friendships and my marriage. Let's just say a lack of sleep is never good for someone's patience. Also, my body felt worn, I rarely had motivation, and it felt like all I did was try to catch up on sleep. During shifts that were extra hard, I would pray for strength from the Lord and ask Him for little reminders of His presence with me.

One winter night, I was caring for a patient who had been in the hospital for a few months. She had been through something tragic and heartbreaking that ended up impairing her body. I had taken care of her quite a bit, and on this specific night, she called me into her room because she was feeling anxious. She was breathing fast and had tears streaming down her face, but she was unable to put words to what she was feeling.

I asked, "Is there was anything I can do for you? Anything that will make you feel better?"

She replied, "Can you just rub my head? Like, massage it?"

"Sure!" I said. "Do you want me to put some music on to listen to? It might help to calm your thoughts." As she put her head-phones in, I stood there and began to massage her head.

I started praying and interceding for her. *Lord, please help this sweet patient I am taking care of. You know she's been through so much, and You know what she needs—even when I don't. Lord, I pray that You will be with her, letting Your presence be known. I lay her and her situation at Your feet.*

While I continued to rub her head and intercede for her in prayer, I looked up and saw a lit-up Christmas tree in the corner of the room. As I stared at the tree, a feeling of immense joy came over me. The room was completely dark, and this cute little tree in the corner of the room was lighting up everything around it. The patient began to fall asleep, but I continued to fix my eyes on this tree. I felt the Lord speak to me in that moment, *The closer you are to Me, the brighter I shine through you.*

The tree was set among some things from the patient's home. I could see the items closest to the lit-up tree perfectly. But the items that were farther away were harder to see. The Lord used this to show me that when we are closest to Him, His light shines brightest through us. His light is always within us, but as we draw near to Him, the light becomes more visible to others. As I drew near to the Lord in that moment, He showed me that His light was shining through to this patient who needed Him so desperately.

A lot of people ask me how I do what I do. "How can you see

heartbreaking things daily and be okay? How can you see tragedy and still have joy?" And I say that I truly believe the Lord has
me doing what I am doing for a reason. But on my own strength
I would not be able to do it. If I relied solely on myself, I would
not be okay. I have to rely on the strength of the Lord. I must lay
the situations, traumas, and patients at His feet. I rest in Proverbs
3:5: "Trust in the LORD with all your heart and lean not on your
own understanding." It is not up to me to try to understand why
things happen; it is up to me to trust in the Lord with all of my
heart.

> As we draw near to Him, the light becomes
>
> more visible to others.

The moment I had with that patient was a time when I drew
near to the Lord. I wish I could say that's what I always do, but
there have been many times when I haven't. There have been moments when it felt impossible for me to draw near to God—
instances where the lies of the Enemy won the thoughts of my
mind. It is not easy to choose to draw near to God in moments
that feel dark and hopeless. But, my friend, there is power in the
choice to sit with Jesus during really difficult circumstances. When
our circumstances are dark and we draw near to the One who is
the Light, His light becomes more visible to others through us.

Think about the sun. If you were to start getting closer and
closer to the sun, you would end up on fire. The same goes for
Jesus. The closer you become to Jesus, the more on fire for Jesus
you will be—but in a good way! And it has a ripple effect. The
fire that burns within you will be contagious to those you en-

counter. Let's be people so close to Jesus that it is impossible for His goodness not to flow out of us.

HOW TO DRAW NEAR TO GOD

Let's dive into the six ways we can draw nearer to the Light of the world when everything feels hard or we feel stuck. Although it requires work and intentionality on our part, He is worthy of our discipline to get to know Him. He deserves everything we can give to Him, and by leaning on Him in times of darkness we will be strengthened and equipped to shine His light to those around us.

1. INTENTIONALLY READ GOD'S WORD

I truly don't think this can ever be said enough: *God's Word changes everything.* Maybe you've found yourself thinking, *The Bible is boring, I don't understand it, I don't have time for it,* or *I'll read it later.* (I admit, these are thoughts I have had and sometimes still have.) But I want to ask you this hard question: Truly, what in your life should ever have a higher priority than reading the active and living Word of God?

We make long lists of excuses. We spend time doing things like scrolling on social media, watching the news, and working before reading the Bible. We put things that don't add anything to our lives eternally ahead of the one thing that will. The question I have asked myself—and have even asked God—is, *Why? Why is it so hard to put reading my Bible first in my life?* And then, *How do I put the Bible first in my life?*

One thing I want to note is that reading the Bible isn't supposed to feel like a chore or an item to cross off a to-do list. Reading the Bible is for our good. It is where we get to encounter the powerful Word of God, and it is one of the ways He speaks to us. Why would we not want to be in a constant process of communicating with God, allowing Him to build us up and refine us? What makes us think that things in this world should have a higher priority than the one thing that gives us life?

Well, by now, I am sure you can tell what the answer is: *Satan.* The last thing that the Enemy wants is for us to put God's Word first in our lives. So he does everything in his power to distract us, lie to us, and make us feel like it is okay to not make the Bible a priority.

But we can actively fight against these lies and distractions by becoming people who make knowing and reading the Bible a priority. Drawing closer to God means drawing closer to His Word. He reveals Himself and His character to us through His Word.

But we must recognize that we cannot do this on our own. We need to pray and ask the Lord to help us overcome the Enemy's distractions, lies, and temptations. If we come to God daily and ask Him to strengthen us to read His Word, He will help us. In 1 John, it says, "This is the confidence we have in approaching God: that if we ask anything according to his will, he hears us."[1] Reading our Bibles is 100 percent the will of God for our lives, so if we ask Him to strengthen us to do it daily, we can have confidence that He hears our requests.

I think one of the biggest distractions is our phones (eek). We wake up, turn off the alarm, and quickly check texts, emails, the news, and social media. We will talk in more detail in chapter 10 about ways you can set boundaries on the amount of time you spend on social media and phone apps. But one idea for how you can use your phone for good is to set a recurring reminder that says something like "Have you read the most important thing in the world yet today?" or "Have you prioritized the one thing that should have priority in your life?" or "Read the truth that sets you free!"

It is an everyday battle against the Enemy, but I want to remind you that our God has already claimed victory. Stand confident in the One who can help you fight your battles.

2. SIT IN HIS PRESENCE

Sitting silently in the presence of the Lord can be really hard for most people. We are a generation who always has to be doing something, making progress, or tuning out our thoughts. But what if sitting in the silence with our thoughts is right where God wants to meet us? Sometimes, to hear from God we have to silence the noise of the world.

I once did an exercise with a group of women that really helped me slow down and sit in God's presence. We spent fifteen minutes in silence, beginning that time by asking for a characteristic of the Lord, a Bible verse, or a word to sit with. We then focused on what the Lord revealed to us. My focus was on the words *Jesus, You are beautiful.* For fifteen minutes I said *Jesus, You are beautiful* over and over in my mind with a posture to receive whatever the Lord had for me. During this exercise, I felt complete peace and was in awe of how truly beautiful Jesus is.

This exercise wasn't an easy one. Sitting in silence in a room full of people was very challenging because there were many distractions. But as my friend led us through this exercise, she reminded us that our thoughts would most likely begin to drift and that we must have grace for ourselves and then re-center our thoughts when we realized they had strayed. I found this exercise to be a powerful and tangible way to get in the presence of the Lord. I want to challenge you to try it this week. Set aside fifteen minutes and get in His presence!

3. Spend Time in Prayer

The Lord hears us when we speak to Him in prayer. We can bring all our hurts, worries, desires, longings, and pleas to His feet. He wants to show us His love and comfort through it all. We can ask God for anything, but it is when we ask according to His will that we can be confident He will answer us. In the Bible it says, "And we are confident that he hears us whenever we ask for anything that pleases him. And since we know he hears us when we make our requests, we also know that he will give us what we ask for" (1 John 5:14–15, NLT).

You can pray in multiple ways. Here are some of my personal favorites.

Pray the Psalms

I love to pray through the book of Psalms. This is a great way to communicate with God when you are struggling to put thoughts into words. Most of the psalms are already prayers written by others, and it feels very empowering to offer up the same declarations and requests that people like King David prayed to God. The Psalms are a part of God's Word, so it is also very powerful when we make that choice to pray them—and any scripture— over our lives. The Bible is alive, active, and aligned with the heart of the Lord, so we can stand confident in the fact that God hears our prayers when we pray His Word.

Pray the Lord's Prayer

The Lord's Prayer, also known as the "Our Father," is found in Matthew 6, where Jesus is teaching His disciples how they ought to pray. The Lord's Prayer may be very familiar to you—many churches include it in their weekly services. Perhaps you even memorized it when you were young. The unfortunate downside of things becoming overly familiar is that we often tend to recite the words without really thinking about the message. Sometimes our focus is on saying the right words in the right order instead of letting those words transform our hearts or thoughts, and then they become just empty words. I've had to overcome that struggle personally! But when I really stopped to consider that this prayer is what Jesus used to teach His own disciples to pray, and truly examined the message of each line, it made all the difference to me.

I want to share each line of the Lord's Prayer (Matthew 6:9–13) with you so that you can not only understand the intent but also know how to use the principle in your own prayers.

Verse 9: "Our Father in heaven, hallowed be your name." As we open in prayer, we are to first and foremost give praise to God. In my own prayers, I often begin by telling God who He is to me and thanking Him for that.

Verse 10: "Your kingdom come, your will be done, on earth as it is in heaven." We are to recognize that it is not *our* will to be done, but *His* will. This is a time to hand over to the Lord the things we are holding on to and declare that His will be done on earth and in our lives, just as it is in heaven. It also is a time to ask the Lord for His kingdom to reign down here on earth.

Verse 11: "Give us today our daily bread." God provides our every need. He is *Jehovah Jireh*, meaning that He is the God who provides.[2] As we say this sentence, we are declaring and asking that the Lord give us the things that are vital to our lives.

Verse 12: "And forgive us our debts, as we also have forgiven our debtors." As the Lord forgives us, we are to forgive others. This is a time where we can come before the Lord and repent of any sins that need repentance. It also is a time that we can ask the Lord for the strength to forgive those who have wronged us and for help to love and forgive them as He does.

Verse 13: "And lead us not into temptation, but deliver us from the evil one." As the prayer ends, we ask the Lord to help us not be tempted and keep the Enemy away from us. This can be a time of praying for protection from temptation and from Satan's influence over you and over those that you love.

Pray Boldly

Prayer has completely changed my life since I began to ask God very specific requests. When we come before Him in boldness, knowing He is *fully capable* of doing anything we ask, it shows our faith in Him. Does this mean He is obligated to give us everything we ask for—or that we shouldn't believe in Him if He doesn't answer our prayers in the way we want? No! We need to recognize that His answers to our prayers must align with His will, which is always for our own (eventual!) good.

My faith has increased so much since I began to write down specific prayers and then trust that the Lord will do what He wants and what He thinks is best. If His answer is different from what I requested, it doesn't mean He is less powerful. It means He has a different plan that I'm not always called to understand. We can trust His omniscience and His eternal perspective. And if He does do what I pray for, it only increases my faith so much more because it reminds me that I am praying in accordance with His will. But the important thing is that I prayed and asked.

Don't be afraid to pray bold prayers.

A book that has completely changed and encouraged my prayer life is *Draw the Circle* by Mark Batterson. In it, he says, "Maybe our normal is so subnormal that normal seems abnormal. Maybe we need a new normal. Bold prayers and big dreams are normal. Anything less is subnormal. And when bold prayers become the norm, so do the miraculous breakthroughs that follow."[3]

Don't be afraid to pray bold prayers. Don't be afraid to ask for the impossible. Don't be afraid to let the Lord see all the emotions that you are feeling.

4. PLUG INTO A CHURCH COMMUNITY

We were made for community! We were not created to try to do this life alone. But I understand that it can be really hard and intimidating to get involved in a church. For multiple years while I was in college, I kept church hopping, trying to find a church that I liked, where I felt I belonged. Unfortunately, I discovered that I was trying to find a church that *served me* best. That mindset doesn't align well with the healthy church blueprint that the book of Acts in the New Testament gives us. When Acts was written, people were not asking themselves, *What church best serves me?* They were asking questions more like, *How can I best serve? How can I create a community that the Lord wants His church to be?*

To get plugged into a church, we first need to start attending church with our eyes open to what is going on around us, looking for places where we can contribute. We need to take the initiative to plug ourselves in. I talk to a lot of people who attend churches and say that no one has come up to them yet and invited them to something. If that is you right now, I want to challenge you to not wait for someone to come up to you! Instead, jump in head-first and see how God shows up when you choose to be a part of His beautiful church. (I do also understand that there can be deep church hurt. That is something to lay at the feet of Jesus; ask Him how He wants you to go about moving forward.)

If you are currently attending a church, ask yourself how you could best use your gifts to serve the Lord. If you aren't attending a church, I challenge you to ask a friend if you can go with them. Or do some research to find a church near you to try yourself! Going to a new church can surely be uncomfortable. But, remember, as Christians we are not called to live a comfortable life.

5. MARVEL AT GOD'S CREATION

As I am writing this, I am sitting outside at a coffee shop. I can feel the breeze tickle the hair on my arm. The sun is hiding behind some fog but starting to make its way out. Its heat feels like a big warm hug. The trees are green and full of beauty, and I can hear sweet little birds singing songs in the distance. The people around me are talking about their families and how much they adore them.

I take a deep breath in and acknowledge that God is with me in this very moment as I am writing. And God is with you in this very moment as you are reading.

Take note of your own surroundings right now. What are you feeling? What are you seeing? What are you smelling? What are you hearing? What are you tasting? Take the time to acknowledge all of the senses the Lord so beautifully blessed us with. Not only is the Lord with us in every moment, but He also intentionally created the world we experience Him in. Think about the things that make you come alive. Think about your favorite activities. Where do those things take place? What is special about where they take place? How can you take the time to recognize the intentionality of the Lord in them?

It wasn't a coincidence that the Lord made Mount Everest. He didn't create all the seasons we see, feel, and experience "just because." It wasn't random that we each grew and developed in our mother's womb. God was intentional with every single thing He created. When we take the time to remember how big and powerful our God truly is, it causes us to stand in awe of Him. It reminds us that we are so small in comparison to who He is, what He has done, and what He is doing.

6. SPEND TIME IN WORSHIP

The last way to draw near to Jesus we are going to cover is through worship. My husband always says, "God, You are deserving of our best praise on our worst day." I love that. The Lord is always deserving of our praise and worship, no matter what our circumstances may be. We must choose to declare God's truth and sovereignty over our lives. Even when it feels so hard to say things like "You are good," the Lord sees your faith.

What even is worship? I think we often associate worship with singing songs in church on a Sunday morning. And while that is a huge part of what worship is, it doesn't end there. We can also worship in a lot of other ways. To worship is to express reverence.[4] Worship is taking the time to recognize God for all that He is and does. We can express reverence for Him through our words, our songs, our thoughts, and our actions. Worship should be our way of life. We can worship at work, we can worship when we do the dishes, we can worship when we are grocery shopping, we can worship when we drive, we can worship when we are in a class. In other words, we have the opportunity to worship every single moment of our days in all that we do.

— ◆ —

These six ways of drawing close to the Lord have changed how I experience and interact with God. I have encountered the Holy Spirit in new, beautiful ways. I have no doubt that if you incorporate some of these practices into your daily, weekly, or monthly routines, you, too, will grow closer to God. He is always near to us, but we decide how near we let ourselves get to Him.

Let's look at the story of Moses and see how when he drew near to the Lord, he reflected God's radiance.

LET GOD'S GLORY RADIATE FROM YOU

Moses's story in the Bible shows us what it means to draw near to the Light and shine brightly. In Exodus 3:1–12, an angel of the Lord appears to Moses from within a burning bush:

> Now Moses was tending the flock of Jethro his father-in-law, the priest of Midian, and he led the flock to the far side of the wilderness and came to Horeb, the mountain of God. There the angel of the Lord appeared to him in flames of fire from within a bush. Moses saw that though the bush was on fire it did not burn up. So Moses thought, "I will go over and see this strange sight—why the bush does not burn up."
>
> When the Lord saw that he had gone over to look, God called to him from within the bush, "Moses! Moses!"
>
> And Moses said, "Here I am."
>
> "Do not come any closer," God said. "Take off your sandals, for the place where you are standing is holy ground." Then he said, "I am the God of your father, the God of Abraham, the God of Isaac and the God of Jacob." At this, Moses hid his face, because he was afraid to look at God.
>
> The Lord said, "I have indeed seen the misery of my people in Egypt. I have heard them crying out because of their slave drivers, and I am concerned about their suffering. So I have come down to rescue them from the hand of the Egyptians

and to bring them up out of that land into a good and spacious land, a land flowing with milk and honey—the home of the Canaanites, Hittites, Amorites, Perizzites, Hivites and Jebusites. And now the cry of the Israelites has reached me, and I have seen the way the Egyptians are oppressing them. So now, go. I am sending you to Pharaoh to bring my people the Israelites out of Egypt."

But Moses said to God, "Who am I that I should go to Pharaoh and bring the Israelites out of Egypt?"

And God said, "I will be with you. And this will be the sign to you that it is I who have sent you: When you have brought the people out of Egypt, you will worship God on this mountain."

God appears to Moses in the form of *light*. And He then calls Moses to bring the people out of Egypt. A huge task to complete. And Moses's response was to ask, "Who am I?" You may have that response to the call on your life: *But, Lord, who am I?*

Take a look at what the Lord's response back to Moses was: "I will be with you." My friend, in everything you do, the Lord is with you. You may be doubting your call. You may feel disqualified to go and be a light for Christ. You may not even want to do it. But the Lord will be with you. That is a promise from God. It's a reminder that you aren't called to do any of this holy work alone but rather alongside the Father.

When you draw near to the Lord,

His radiance shines from you.

As the story of Moses continues in Exodus, this prophecy of God comes true: "And this will be the sign to you that it is I who have sent you: When you have brought the people out of Egypt, you will worship God on this mountain" (verse 12). Fast-forward to Exodus 34. To set the scene, Moses is back on Mount Sinai, and the Lord has him remake the two stone tablets that have the Ten Commandments written on them. It is written:

> When Moses came down Mount Sinai carrying the two stone tablets inscribed with the terms of the covenant, he wasn't aware that his face had become radiant because he had spoken to the LORD. So when Aaron and the people of Israel saw the radiance of Moses' face, they were afraid to come near him.
>
> But Moses called out to them and asked Aaron and all the leaders of the community to come over, and he talked with them. Then all the people of Israel approached him, and Moses gave them all the instructions the LORD had given him on Mount Sinai. When Moses finished speaking with them, he covered his face with a veil. But whenever he went into the Tent of Meeting to speak with the LORD, he would remove the veil until he came out again. Then he would give the people whatever instructions the LORD had given him, and the people of Israel would see the radiant glow of his face. So he would put the veil over his face until he returned to speak with the LORD. (Exodus 34:29–35, NLT)

Moses was not aware that his face became radiant from speaking to the Lord. His face was literally shining. Beaming with light so bright that it frightened those around him.

My friend, when you do anything with the Lord—when you spend time with Him, speak to Him, or pray to Him—you become radiant. When you draw near to the Lord, His radiance shines from you.

MAKE HIS LIGHT VISIBLE

All of these ways to draw near to the Lord are so important to our relationship with Him. But I also recognize that examining all six ways could possibly feel overwhelming. God isn't telling you, *Do all of these today or else you will not shine!* No, no, no, that is not the heart of the Lord. I challenge you to think of maybe one or two of these areas that you want to focus on. Ask the Lord how He is calling you to draw closer to Him. As you begin to implement a few things into your daily life, continue to ask what more the Lord has for you.

Maybe you already do some of these things. Maybe you haven't ever done any, and that is okay. The Lord is not condemning you for that, but rather He says, *My child, I have so much for you, and I want to show it to you.*

I want to close this chapter with a prayer that you can refer to as you start or continue on a journey of drawing close to the Lord.

Lord, I come before You today with a heart eager to draw closer to You. I have the desire to be a bright, shining light for You and only You. I want to know more about You. I want to understand Your heart for me, for others, and for this world. What is an area of my life You are calling me to seek more of You in? How do You want me to draw near to You? I cannot do this alone. I need Your strength and Your grace. Lord, I ask for help to fight the lies of the Enemy that want to distract me away from You. Protect me, guide me, and teach me more about Yourself. Make me more like

You. Help me to draw closer to You so that Your light becomes more visible through me to those around me. I want my face to be radiant like the face of Moses after he spent time with You. Amen.

ARISE AND SHINE

- What is one thing you can do in this very moment to draw closer to the Lord?
- Think of a friend or person in your life who visibly shines so bright for Christ. Invite her to coffee and ask her what her walk with the Lord looks like.
- As much as I want you to read this book, reading the Bible is even more important! Spend time with God right now and come back to this tomorrow.

7

PIERCING PRAISE

Worshipping Wholeheartedly
When It Feels Impossible

IT WAS A FRIDAY, and I had picked up an extra shift at the hospital. It had luckily been a pretty slow and easy morning for me, so I walked to the nurse break room to check my phone. I opened my locker, grabbed my phone out of my backpack, and texted my husband to ask him how his day was. He responded, "I think I am getting let go from my job." Instantly my heart started pounding, my hands began sweating, and my mind went into panic mode. That was the last thing I had expected to hear from him. I immediately called him to ask for the details, and I could hear the trembling fear in his voice. My husband told me that he was about to have a meeting with his boss where he would find out if it was actually happening or not. Those next thirty minutes felt like three days to me. I could hardly focus on the work I was doing and began to think of all of the worst outcomes. Thirty minutes passed by. I went to check my phone again and saw the text, "It happened."

Instantly my mind began to question the Lord. *What is going on? Why would this happen, Lord? My husband loves his job as a recruiter and is so happy. Why would such a good thing be taken away?* On top of all these questions, I began to panic about our finances. The Lord had been doing a lot of work in my life ministry-wise and had called me to cut down the hours I was working at the hospital. I had been in my new schedule for only a few weeks. So not only was my husband's income now gone, but it was also the income that we were depending on at that time. *How are we going to make it?* I began to spiral into overwhelm with worry of the future.

I got home from work that night and wrapped my arms around my husband. We held each other and cried, confused and upset at what had happened that day. We know God is good. We know He has the best for us. But at that moment, it was really hard to declare. We reached out to friends and family for prayer because we knew that the journey ahead was one that we couldn't do alone. We needed help remembering the truth that the Lord declares over us. We asked our friends to intercede for us to help us fight the lies that the Enemy was trying to make us believe.

It is about declaring what we know to be true

despite what we feel.

Two days later was Sunday. My husband is the worship leader at the church we attend. I was brought to tears watching him still choose to wholeheartedly worship the Lord even through some very difficult circumstances. He chose to declare light over the situation in his life that felt very dark. He chose to sing praise to God when it was difficult.

A sacrifice takes place when we choose to declare God's truth over the hard, gut-wrenching, heart-breaking situations that happen in our lives. That Sunday my husband said to our church congregation, "God is deserving of our best praise on our worst day." As I mentioned in the last chapter, that's a line he says frequently, but to see him actively live it out gave it so much more power. Our circumstances do not change the fact that God is good, God is faithful, God is powerful, and God is all-knowing. It honors Him when we declare the truth of who He is over our hard circumstances. It isn't about what we feel when it comes to Jesus. It is about declaring what we know to be true despite what we feel.

A friend encouraged me with a verse in the middle of the confusion we were feeling, and I share it to encourage you today if you are in a similar season: "For the LORD God is a sun and shield; the LORD bestows favor and honor. No good thing does he withhold from those who walk uprightly" (Psalm 84:11, ESV).

When we are walking uprightly with the Lord, He does not withhold good from us, even though we may have to wait for things to happen. If you are in a long waiting season or one that has come out of nowhere, just keep reminding yourself, *No good thing is God withholding from me. I will worship Him in the waiting.*

WORSHIP IN THE IMPOSSIBLE

Let's look at a story from the Bible where worship was used as a weapon against the Enemy to declare the truth of who God is, despite the circumstances. Spoiler alert: Satan was defeated.

In 2 Chronicles 20, multiple large armies declared war on King Jehoshaphat. This terrified him (I mean who wouldn't be terrified?). But Jehoshaphat turned to God and pleaded for guidance. In fact, King Jehoshaphat ordered that everyone in Judah fast and also seek the Lord's help. Jehoshaphat then stood before all of Judah and prayed and declared the truth of who God was to them, saying:

> You are the ruler of all the kingdoms of the earth. You are powerful and mighty; no one can stand against you! . . . We can cry out to you to save us, and you will hear us and rescue us. . . . O our God, won't you stop them? We are powerless against this mighty army that is about to attack us. We do not know what to do, but we are looking to you for help. (verses 6, 9, 12, NLT)

Wow, what faith it takes to declare those words when a daunting situation is before you that puts your own life at risk. Yet that is what King Jehoshaphat did. And it wasn't in secret and by himself; it was amid all the people of Judah. His faith led their faith.

As all the people of Judah (including women and children) were gathered around King Jehoshaphat, the Spirit of the Lord came upon a man named Jahaziel standing in the crowd. He said,

> Listen, all you people of Judah and Jerusalem! Listen, King Jehoshaphat! This is what the LORD says: Do not be afraid! Don't be discouraged by this mighty army, for the battle is not yours, but God's. Tomorrow, march out against them. You will find them coming up through the ascent of Ziz at the end of the valley that opens into the wilderness of Jeruel. But you will not even need to fight. Take your positions; then stand still and watch the LORD's victory. He is with you, O people of Judah and Jerusalem. Do not be afraid or discouraged. Go out against them tomorrow, for the LORD is with you! (2 Chronicles 20:15–17, NLT)

Immediately after Jahaziel spoke these words, King Jehosha-phat knelt and put his face to the ground. All of Judah and Jeru-salem then joined in and began to worship and sing praise to the Lord. They chose to worship not because of what was happening in their lives but because of who God was to them.

The next morning Jehoshaphat and the army of Judah went out into the wilderness as the Lord told them to. Not only did they obey the Lord, but they also had faith that He would deliver them from what seemed like the most impossible situation. While they were on the way into the wilderness, Jehoshaphat stopped them and said, "Listen to me, all you people of Judah and Jerusalem! Believe in the LORD your God, and you will be able to stand firm. Believe in his prophets, and you will succeed" (2 Chronicles 20:20, NLT).

The king then proceeded to appoint people to walk ahead of the army of Judah and sing to the Lord. They sang, "Give thanks to the LORD; his faithful love endures forever!" (2 Chronicles 20:21, NLT).

There is so much power in what was about to take place for all of Judah:

At the very moment they began to sing and give praise, the LORD caused the armies of Ammon, Moab, and Mount Seir to start fighting among themselves. The armies of Moab and Ammon turned against their allies from Mount Seir and killed every one of them. After they had destroyed the army of Seir, they began attacking each other. So when the army of Judah arrived at the lookout point in the wilderness, all they saw were dead bodies lying on the ground as far as they could see. Not a single one of the enemy had escaped. (2 Chronicles 20:22–24, NLT)

That's amazing!

At the very moment that the army began to sing worship to the Lord, God went before them and caused the armies coming after Judah to begin attacking each other! I have goosebumps on my skin and tears filling my eyes as I type out these words. Nothing can stand against our God. And there is more power than we will ever know in our words when we choose to praise the Lord amid our hard circumstances. The God of Jehoshaphat is your God!

Okay, the story isn't even over yet.

After King Jehoshaphat and his men arrived at the scene where the armies lay dead, they went to gather the plunder. They came across ample equipment, clothing, and other valuables—so much that they couldn't even carry it all back at one time. It took them multiple days to gather it all. Not only did the Lord go before them and fight for them, but He also provided for them above and beyond what they could have even imagined.

This story has the goodness and power of God written all over it. I'll say it again: *The God who defeated those armies is your God.* So, what battle lies ahead of you that seems impossible? What feels so dark to you? Is it a marriage that seems too hard to stay in? Is it a strained relationship with a friend? Is it a child who is in and out of jail? Is it your job that you feel stuck in? Is it church hurt? Is it fear of failure? Is it the inability to keep up with the pressures of this world?

Whatever you are going through, I challenge you to sing and give praise to God. Not because you are happy about your circumstances (although we are called to rejoice in our sufferings, which is a whole other topic in itself) but because of who God is. King Jehoshaphat and all of Judah had envisioned an outcome where they would most likely be defeated by these armies. They didn't have much hope according to worldly eyes. But they placed their hope and faith in Jesus. They declared the truth of who He is over their circumstances. And look at what happened!

> When we sing praise to Him, the light can't
>
> help but infiltrate every dark area.

I also want to mention that we don't worship God just to get something from Him. That mindset is rooted in pride. We are not deserving of anything, but because of the loving heart of God, in Jesus, we are given more than we could ever merit. That is why we give praise. That is why we declare who God is over our circumstances. Sometimes our situations don't change, or they go in a direction we don't want. But still, that does not have anything to do with the goodness of God. Rather, it has everything to do with the fact that we live in a fallen world. We have to remember that we cannot trust in the things of this world; we have to set our hope on the things above. We are going to have trials and suffering in this life. There is darkness around us, but that darkness has not won, and it will not win. The light of Christ wins every single day. In Jesus we are victorious because of the hope that is for us in heaven. When we sing praise to Him, the light can't help but infiltrate every dark area.

PRAISE THAT BREAKS CHAINS

Let's explore one more Bible story where God's power reigned down because of worship. In Acts 16, the Holy Spirit led Paul and Silas to Macedonia. At a place of prayer, they met a young woman who was a slave. There was a spirit inside her that wasn't from God but was from Satan. This spirit enabled the slave girl to tell the future, and her masters used her as a fortune teller to make them a lot of money. After a few days of being with this girl, Paul commanded the demon to come out of her—and it did. After this, her masters were so upset with Paul and Silas for what they did (since the girl could no longer tell fortunes and make money), they commanded city officials to throw them into prison. Before being imprisoned, Paul and Silas were severely beaten by a mob at the direction of the officials.[1]

The Bible continues, "Around midnight Paul and Silas were praying and singing hymns to God, and the other prisoners were listening" (Acts 16:25, NLT).

What would your first reaction be if you were beaten for doing something the Holy Spirit prompted you to do? What if you were then thrown into prison for it? Paul and Silas chose to worship amid their crazy circumstances. Their faith at this moment inspires me so much.

Then after they began to worship the Lord an amazing thing happened: "Suddenly, there was a massive earthquake, and the prison was shaken to its foundations. All the doors immediately flew open, and the chains of every prisoner fell off! The jailer woke up to see the prison doors wide open" (Acts 16:26–27, NLT).

The praise that Paul and Silas were singing caused the chains of every prisoner to break (insert mind-blown emoji)! It wasn't power from Paul and Silas; it was the power of God. But Paul and Silas chose to worship despite the challenging situation *because of their faith*. They declared the truth of who God was to them and actively fought against the schemes of the Enemy. As we see in this scene, the Enemy tried to win but was defeated by the power of our God.

These two stories are not accidentally in the Bible. They are there to show us the power of our worship. We may not personally witness enemy armies attacking each other or the ground shaking and chains breaking (although we could, because we cannot limit God!). But when we choose to sing praise to God, His power is activated. And God's power is victorious over the Enemy every single second of every day.

Your situation doesn't change who God is; God changes the situation you are in. Invite Him into it.

What do you feel chained to? What seems like a giant standing in your way? What looks too dark in your life to have light in it? What feels broken? What feels too lost to be found? Whatever your answers are to those questions, I want to challenge you to worship through them. I am not saying to belittle the situations or pretend they aren't there. Rather, declare who God is over them. Remember: Our circumstances have nothing to do with whether God is powerful or not. God *is* powerful. God is good. God is almighty. Your situation doesn't change who God is; God changes the situation you are in. Invite Him into it.

WORSHIP WITH ALL THAT YOU ARE

In the book *Holy Roar*, Chris Tomlin tells a story of himself and some Christian friends at a U2 concert. He mentioned how at church, these guys were more on the reserved side when they sang worship. But when the U2 concert began, these same friends all jammed to the songs that took them back to their middle school days. Hands raised, they were screaming out the lyrics, jumping up and down, completely sold out. The next day Chris reflected on the concert, "In church when they sang about Jesus— his life, death, and resurrection—when they sang about their own freedom, what was keeping them from offering just as much enthusiasm? Shouldn't they be even more effusive in those moments of praise?"[2]

I've noticed this in my own friends, my family, and even myself. At a concert we readily sing at the top of our lungs, jump up and down with joy, and raise our hands so high. We sing along and exert so much of our energy for bands that have done nothing significant for us except maybe entertain us. Then, when it comes to singing in church to the One who laid His life down for us because He loves us, we often stand still and merely lip-synch the words. *What keeps us from giving all of our worship to Him?*

Don't hold back because you feel embarrassed or uncomfortable. Would you hold back at your favorite band's concert if everyone around you was singing and dancing? Give Jesus your first and your best. He is deserving of that and more.

WORSHIP WHENEVER, WHEREVER

Worshipping God doesn't happen only in a church building at nine o'clock on Sunday morning. Worship is a way of life. As we touched on a bit in the previous chapter, worshipping is expressing reverence for something. We can express reverence to the Lord through anything we do. In case you're like me and need to hear tangible ideas to implement something new, I want to share with you some ways to incorporate more worship in your life.

An easy way to incorporate worship is to listen to worship music while you drive. When you are by yourself in the car, taking the kids to school, or on a road trip with your spouse or friends, throw on some worship music. You don't need to have a special aesthetic place to worship the Lord. Jesus wasn't about burning a candle, having the lighting right, or playing instrumental music in the background to set the mood. He chose to worship everywhere He went and modeled it for other people.

Moms, your kids will remember the days that you were worshipping the Lord in the car as you drove them to school. Women, your friends may not know the truth of the Lord, but what if they heard it as you sang along to the song playing in your car? The car is also a great place to sing unabashedly when you are driving alone. You can let all the walls down. There is no one listening to you; it's just you and the Lord. Talk to Him out loud. Sing out loud. It can feel uncomfortable at first, but soon you will look forward to those car rides where you can just have a conversation with Jesus as if He is a best friend in your passenger seat (because He is!).

My husband and I chose to worship together at home one night a few weeks after he lost his recruiting job. My husband played his piano, and we stood in our living room and praised the Lord. We sang words that were easy to say but hard to believe. We clung to the truth as tightly as we could. In this hard season when he was between jobs (a few months that felt like a year), we saw God provide for us in ways we couldn't imagine. In a time when we should have felt financially stressed, we didn't. Our finances didn't make sense. Our marriage was stronger than ever. And, praise the Lord, my husband was able to find a new job in the Lord's perfect time. Our worship amid the confusion brought us closer together and closer to the Lord in that season. Now, looking back, I love what the Lord did in our hearts during that uncertain time.

We can also worship the Lord in the very mundane moments

of our lives. Again, worship is showing reverence to God. As you wash the dishes, you can worship: *Thank You, Lord, for providing food to eat, thank You for what You have done for my family, and thank You for who You are to me.* The same goes for when you are doing laundry: *Thank You, Lord, for giving me everything I need. Thank You for clothing me. Thank You for soap to clean my clothes. Thank You, Lord, for dry clothes.* Giving thanks to God is worshipping Him because it is declaring who He is. When we give thanks and have gratitude for even the smallest things, our hearts shift toward a posture of joy.

In Ann Voskamp's *One Thousand Gifts Devotional,* she touches on how our joy is dependent on the depths of our thanks:

"And he took bread, *gave thanks* and broke it, and gave it to them" (Luke 22:19, emphasis added).

I read it slowly. In the original language, "he gave thanks" reads "*eucharisteo.*" I underline it on the page.

The root word of *eucharisteo* is *charis,* meaning "grace." Jesus took the bread and saw it as grace and gave thanks. He took the bread and knew it to be *gift* and gave thanks.

But there is more, and I read it. *Eucharisteo,* thanksgiving, envelopes the Greek word for grace, *charis.* But it also holds its derivative, the Greek word *chara,* meaning "joy." *Joy.* . . . That might be what the quest for more is all about—that which Augustine claimed, "Without exception . . . all try their hardest to reach the same goal, that is joy." . . .

That's what I was struggling to reach, to seize. Joy. But where can I seize this holy grail of joy? I look back down to the page. Was this the clue to the quest of all most important? Deep *chara* joy is found only at the table of the *euCHARisteo*— the table of thanksgiving. I sit there long . . . wondering . . . is it that simple?

Is the height of my *chara* joy dependent on the depths of my *eucharisteo* thanks?

So then as long as thanks is possible—I think this through—as long as thanks is possible, then joy is always possible.[3]

In the mundane, everyday moments, when we choose to worship and give thanks to the Lord, we can find joy. *We will find joy.*

Finally, we can worship through the work we do. Whatever we are doing, God is working in it. Maybe you are a lawyer, a teacher, a nurse, a physical therapist, a nanny, a graphic designer, or a bus driver. Whatever it is you do, in all that you do, do it for the glory of the Lord. Worship Him in the middle of your work. That can look different depending on what you do. But when you recognize the Lord in whatever you do, that is worship. In the mornings, or whenever you go into work, ask the Lord to help you see where He is throughout your day. Recognize Him in the big ways and in the small ways. Ask Him to help you slow down so you don't miss what He has in store for you.

There are so many ways we can worship the Lord. No darkness can overcome the light of Jesus. When we declare His truth—His light—over what may seem like a very dark situation to us, that situation does not win. Those chains no longer have a hold on you because of what Jesus has done on the cross for you. Speak the truth of who He is over every area in your life, even if it is hard. Even when it feels impossible to say the words, make the choice to say them. Even when it hurts to think about what you are going through, choose to declare who Jesus is over it. Jesus has won, my friend. You don't have any more fighting to do. Let Him fight for you. Let Him go before you. Let Him be your strength and your shield. Let His light infiltrate every area of your life as you choose to worship Him.

ARISE AND SHINE

- The next time you are in church worshipping, give it your all. Give Jesus your all.
- Write a list of gratitude to the Lord. Thank Him for the littlest things. Joy comes from thanksgiving.
- What is one way that you can worship the Lord today?

8

ARMOR OF LIGHT

Putting on the Armor of God to Fight Against the Darkness

A NOTE FROM ALLYSON: *Before you read the following story, I want to acknowledge the possibility that some may be sensitive to the content. One of my dearest friends is allowing me to share her experience with pregnancy loss. I tell this story with the awareness of the feelings it could possibly bring up for you if you have had a similar hardship. My prayer is that you can see and experience what Jesus has for you amid trials. I hope that wherever you are, my friend's story shows you a little glimpse of God's goodness and light amid grief and darkness. However, if you want to skip this chapter, please do so and I'll see you in chapter 9!*

IT WAS AT THE end of 2019, and I had recently become friends with a girl named Kaity. Our personalities clicked, and we became good friends fast. She had just moved to California from Kentucky with her husband, and they had gotten plugged into the church that my husband and I attend. She began attending a women's group that I also went to, which is where our friendship began to grow. Her faith inspired me. Her love for Jesus was so apparent, it radiated off of her onto everyone she met. During one of our ladies' nights, Kaity told some of us that she was pregnant. We were all so excited for her and this new adventure of motherhood she was about to embark on.

Sadly, a few weeks later I sat with Kaity in her grief as she walked through some pregnancy complications and ultimately lost her baby. Grief is so hard to bear—and so hard to watch someone experience. Kaity was heartbroken and devastated. She questioned God as she was going through one of the darkest and hardest times of her life. This moment of loss impacted Kaity's life so deeply and was something she had to learn to navigate with her husband, family, and friends.

I interviewed Kaity for this chapter a few years after she walked through that incredibly hard season, after she had a lot of time to process what she experienced. I asked her how she tangibly chose the hope of Jesus during the hardest moment of her life, and she said something that deeply encouraged me; I pray it encourages you too. She said, "I was at a point where I could lean in or lean out. I thought, *If I lean out, what will that look like and where will that lead me? But if I lean in, what will that look like and where could that lead me?*" She continued, "When we walk through grief, we have the choice to *press into* the Lord or to isolate and *retreat away from* the Lord."

She talked about some lyrics that we recently sang in church. The lyrics go, "I give to you all that I am, all that I was, and all that I will be. I lay it at your feet."[1] (This song was written by my husband!) She said that as she was reading and singing those lyrics in church, she started to think about how there is not one thing good or bad, hard or easy, sad or joyful, that she has laid at Jesus's feet that He hasn't done something good with. Her words were, "Anytime I have surrendered my pain or joy to Jesus—any part of me—it has always actually turned out good."

When Kaity was walking through this deep grief and despair, she found herself in the book of Job. Job lived a very difficult life full of pain and destruction. Kaity related to him in this loss she was experiencing. But she felt like she had a choice to lay her grief at God's feet and trust that He would redeem it just as He redeemed all of Job's pain. Or she could choose to hang on to her pain and try to do something with her grief on her own. As she considered this, she realized that if she tried to do it on her own, it would only hurt even more and keep her stuck.

At the end of the book of Job, God rescues Job from all of the pain he experienced and restores his life. Job says, "God has delivered me from going down to the pit, and I shall live to enjoy the light of life" (Job 33:28). Likewise, it was through this time of grief in Kaity's life that she chose to remember that Jesus is the light of her life. And it's His light that overcomes all darkness. Kaity chose to fight against the schemes of the Enemy and the darkness she was experiencing. She did this with the light of who Jesus was to her and what she knew about His character. Kaity chose to armor up and fight the battle before her. Romans 13:12 says, "The night is nearly over; the day is almost here. So let us put aside the deeds of darkness and put on the armor of light." Kaity put on the armor of light to fight against the darkness.

When we lean in and put on the armor of light, nothing can defeat us. It's indestructible armor.

The armor of light is related to Jesus Himself. When we put on Jesus, we are equipped to both defend against and attack the Enemy's deeds of darkness.[2] New Testament scholar Leon Morris says, "'Putting on Christ' is a strong and vivid metaphor. It means more than 'put on the character of the Lord Jesus Christ,' signifying rather 'Let Christ Jesus Himself be the armor that you wear.'"[3]

That is the choice we get to make when we face any trial in our lives. We can choose to put on Jesus Christ Himself or we can try to do everything on our own. Friend, depending on our own strength will never work out as well as inviting Jesus into our difficulty. In the hardest of the hard moments and in the deepest grief, Jesus wants to be with you. He wants to fight for you. God didn't create you to do anything on your own. Rather, He intended you to be fully dependent on Him. As my friend Kaity said, we are either leaning into Jesus or we are leaning away from Him. When we lean in and put on the armor of light, nothing can defeat us. *It's indestructible armor.*

ARMOR UP

We live in a world that is dark. That is a fact. We are going to walk through things that are dark. That is also a fact—and not just a modern-day fact but also a biblical fact. And the thing is, darkness is where the Enemy wants you to stay. The Enemy wants you to believe that it is too dark for there to ever be light. The Enemy wants you to have no hope. His strategy is to distract us. His strategy is to lie to us but make it sound like truth. Satan doesn't want us to *fully* understand the fact that the light of Christ is in us.

But you know what is a biblical fact? *Jesus is the light of the world, and whoever follows Him will not walk in darkness but will have the light of life.*[4] So, how do we fight against the strategies of the devil? *We do what God's Word says.* We put on the full armor of God to fight against the evil rulers and authorities of the unseen world:

> A final word: Be strong in the Lord and in his mighty power. Put on all of God's armor so that you will be able to stand firm against all strategies of the devil. For we are not fighting against flesh-and-blood enemies, but against evil rulers and authorities of the unseen world, against mighty powers in this dark world, and against evil spirits in the heavenly places.
>
> Therefore, put on every piece of God's armor so you will be able to resist the enemy in the time of evil. Then after the battle you will still be standing firm. Stand your ground, putting on the belt of truth and the body armor of God's righteousness. For shoes, put on the peace that comes from the Good News so that you will be fully prepared. In addition to all of these, hold up the shield of faith to stop the fiery arrows of the devil. Put on salvation as your helmet, and take the sword of the Spirit, which is the word of God. (Ephesians 6:10–17, NLT)

Picture a soldier who is putting on his armor to go into battle. Essentially, we also must daily put on all the armor of Ephesians 6 to stand firm against the evil forces that are in this world.

This is what my friend Kaity did as she walked through a very dark time in her life. She knew she was in a spiritual battle. She had a choice to make. And she did her best to choose to put on the full armor of God as she battled against the strategies of the Enemy. It was challenging, but she came out on the other side victorious. This is what you can do too. In every area of your life, you have the choice to armor up or fight in your own strength.

Let's dive into each piece of armor mentioned in Ephesians 6 to learn what they mean to us and how we use them to fight against the dark powers in the world.

BELT OF TRUTH

The belt of truth is the first piece of armor mentioned. A belt may not seem like the most important piece, but it is first for a reason. The belt secures every piece of our armor.[5] We must walk in truth in all that we do. In order to fight against the Enemy we must be first rooted in truth, and then everything we do after will flow from that. The belt is also the piece that is closest to the body. We must hold the truth of God close to us so that we can stand against whatever may come our way.

BODY ARMOR OF GOD'S RIGHTEOUSNESS

The body armor of God's righteousness is also called the breast-plate of righteousness. The meaning of *righteousness* in this verse is "the act of doing what is in agreement with God's standards, the state of being in proper relationship with God."[6] A breast-plate didn't cover only the front of the body; it also covered the back.[7] When we put on this breastplate of righteousness, we aren't putting on our own righteousness but the Lord's, which He gives us when we become a new creation in Him. When we say yes to Jesus, our old self is thrown off and we become new. Ephesians 4:22–24 says, "You were taught, with regard to your former way of life, to put off your old self, which is being corrupted by its deceitful desires; to be made new in the attitude of your minds; and to put on the new self, created to be like God in true righteousness and holiness."

Our old self that was rooted in sin has died, and we are now new and righteous in Christ. When we put on His righteousness, the Enemy cannot defeat us because we are no longer fighting on our own strength. Now Christ fights on our behalf.

SHOES OF PEACE

In Ephesians 6, the shoes of peace are easily overlooked. Scripture says, "For shoes, put on the peace that comes from the Good News so that you will be fully prepared."[8] Or, in other words, be ready everywhere you go to share the good news in a peaceful way. The Enemy does not like it when we know the gospel and walk according to the gospel. And he especially doesn't like when we share that gospel with others. When we are walking peacefully, with our heart set on the Great Commission to go and make disciples, that threatens the Enemy.

SHIELD OF FAITH

The firm foundation of our faith will protect us from the fiery arrows of the Enemy (meaning any tactics he tries to send our way to turn us away from Jesus). We can hold on to our faith to protect ourselves from falling into the traps or schemes of the Enemy. Satan threatens us with fear, rejection, darkness, grief, and so many other hard things. Rather than give up and fall for Satan's threats, we get to choose to place our trust and hope in Jesus. Jesus says in Matthew 17:20, "I tell you the truth, if you had faith even as small as a mustard seed, you could say to this mountain, 'Move from here to there,' and it would move. Nothing would be impossible" (NLT). *Faith the size of a mustard seed can move a mountain.* With our faith, the tiniest amount of faith, we can stand tall and strong to fight against the attacks of the Enemy. Without faith it would be impossible to stand against the Enemy, but with our faith nothing is impossible because God works and fights for us.

HELMET OF SALVATION

A helmet is important in any kind of battle or competition. The part it plays in the armor of God is to protect the place where our thoughts stem from—our minds. The helmet helps protect us against discouragement as we fix our minds on the hope of our present and future salvation.[9] Bible teacher David Guzik explains it like this:

> 1 Thessalonians 5:8 speaks of the helmet of salvation in connection to *the hope of salvation*. The helmet of salvation protects us against discouragement, against the desire to give up, giving us hope not only in knowing that we *are* saved, but that we *will be* saved. It is the assurance that God will triumph.
>
> One of Satan's most effective weapons against us is *discouragement*. When we are properly equipped with the helmet of salvation, it's hard to stay discouraged.[10]

It's the helmet that reminds us of who we are and what our purpose is as people who are saved by God.

THE SWORD OF THE SPIRIT

The sword of the Spirit is the Word of God.[11] Let that truth seep deep in your soul for a second. God's Word is literally the one thing that Satan cannot stand against. Who can stand against a sword? It pierces and kills. The sword of the Spirit destroys any lie of the Enemy. And take note here: It is the only offensive piece of the armor of God. Everything else is used for defense, but the sword is the one true weapon we can use to fight back. Hebrews 4:12 also describes God's Word as a sword: "For the word of God is living and active, sharper than any two-edged sword, piercing to the division of soul and of spirit, of joints and of marrow, and discerning the thoughts and intentions of the heart" (ESV).

This isn't just a verse to try to get you to read your Bible. This is biblical truth from God saying that His Word is literally able to fight against the evil powers of this world for us. His Word pierces our hearts and the hearts of others so that we may know and understand His goodness and righteousness. God's Word is the most powerful weapon we have. Just like any other weapon, in order to use it, we must be equipped. We must know His Word to actually wield it. So it's no wonder that the Enemy does everything he can to keep us from reading the Bible.

> Everything else is used for defense, but the sword of the
> Spirit is the one true weapon we can use to fight back.

Ask yourself how often you take the time to get to know God's Word. Maybe you do read your Bible every day, which is incredible! But, for most people, reading the Bible is not a priority in life. I get it; it's so hard, especially with all the things on our to-do lists. A question I have been asking myself, though, when I recognize that I am not putting God's Word first in my life is, *Do I really think the things I need to get done won't happen if God's Word is the true priority in my life?* When we have a big to-do list and Bible reading is on it, it's easy to say, "Oh, I'll just get to that later." And then later comes and it doesn't happen, and we come to the end of another day without reading the truest truth to exist. Know that there is endless grace for you, and God isn't condemning you for this. I just want you to understand that reading your Bible is so powerful, and it is the last thing that the Enemy wants you to do, so he does a good job distracting you with all of these other "important" things. God's Word is your sword. God's Word can tear down any lie of the Enemy. God's Word can transform your life. God's Word is the one weapon that names us victorious when we use it.

PREPARING FOR BATTLE

I recently walked through a battle for my thoughts. It was when I preached for the first time. I was aware that I could possibly encounter spiritual attacks leading up to the event, and thank God for His goodness that I didn't experience anything major. I was in good spirits, I was confident in my calling, and I was excited to see what the Lord was going to do. The night of the women's event came, and it was amazing. So many women received prayer and made the decision to be women who delight in the Lord. God did such beautiful work in the hearts of the women who were at this event, as well as in my own heart.

As I headed home that night, I continued to try to be aware of any attacks of the Enemy. Of course, he hated what had taken place at the event. A few days later I was at work in the hospital when someone came up to me and told me they saw the short video I had posted on Instagram of me preaching. We continued to chat, and then she asked me, "And did you maybe have someone else up there with you, or even in you, as you spoke?" I was confused at first, and then I realized she was asking if I was pregnant. And I definitely wasn't.

My heart sank. That very morning, I had struggled to get my

scrubs on because they were tighter than they used to be on me. I was already feeling so self-conscious and frustrated with how my body was changing, and then this happened. I replied to my co-worker, "Um, actually, no."

She apologized immediately, and I knew it was heartfelt. I said, "It's okay." But I walked away with tears streaming down my face. Thoughts began to pop into my head: *You aren't as beautiful as you want to be. People are noticing your weight gain. You are not as skinny and fit as you used to be.* And the list goes on. The Enemy knew where to attack, and it was really difficult to fight against.

I grabbed my phone and immediately texted my husband, mom, and mother-in-law. I knew I needed help. My mother-in-law responded with, "Ally, the Enemy is trying to attack your identity." As soon as she said that, I realized that I needed to fight back.

I stared at my reflection in the hospital bathroom mirror and began to say over and over in my head, with tear stains on my cheeks, *I am beautiful. I am made in the image of God. I am known. I am loved. I am wonderfully made. The way my body looks does not reflect anything about my heart. Jesus sees me. Jesus knows me. Jesus loves me as I am. My body is beautiful because it was made by my Creator.*

I had to make the choice to fight the lies of the Enemy with the sword of the Spirit. While some of those things I was speaking over myself were very hard to believe at that moment, they were still truths of the Lord. We don't have to fully believe or feel a certain way in order to fight with the truth. Truth is truth. And it's the truth that sets us free. Not only did I choose to use the sword of the Spirit, but I also chose to put on the boots of the gospel of peace.

My co-worker who asked that question pulled me aside later in the shift to sincerely apologize to me. I could have chosen to be mad, hold a grudge, or even retaliate and say something rude back. But I felt a sense of peace. I knew it had been the Enemy at work. So I chose to walk forward in peace and forgive her.

I tell you this story because the Enemy knew how to get me. I had been walking through a season of struggling with my body image. My body was beginning to change as I aged, and I wasn't prioritizing eating healthy or staying active. The Enemy knew that a comment like that could tear me down. He knew it would overshadow the thankfulness I felt about preaching at the women's event and maybe cause me to think twice before accepting another invitation to be on stage. He knew the right button to push in that very moment and season of my life.

> Child of light, it's time to fight
>
> with the armor of light.

When this happens, we have to be ready to fight with the truth of God's Word. We must have all of our armor of light on to help us battle as the Enemy comes to attack us. Every piece works together. And when all the pieces are on and ready for battle, the darkness cannot overcome us.

What about you? Do you know what the Enemy wants to use to attack you? Does he know your weak spot? You can stand strong and fight against the Enemy. Just like my friend Kaity said, it's a choice you have to make. And I don't know about you, but I would rather go into a battle with my armor and sword than without any protection. So, child of light, it's time to fight with the armor of light. Things may be more difficult than you thought, but in Christ, you can't be defeated.

ARISE AND SHINE

- Can you think of a time when the Enemy attacked you in response to something you were doing for the Lord?
- Are you facing a battle now? I encourage you: Armor up!
- Make a list of truths you can fall back on to fight against the lies of the Enemy.

KEEP YOUR EYES ON
THE LIGHTHOUSE

Navigating Grief

MY MOTHER-IN-LAW, BRE, WAS twenty-four when she received a phone call that she was not prepared for. She was taking care of her kids and cleaning her house when her youngest sister, who was about twelve, called to say that their mom had been in the bathroom for a long time and was not responding to her. Bre told her younger sister to go into the bathroom and hand the phone to their mom, but it was obvious that something was not right. As she was now married and had kids of her own, Bre lived in a town eight hours away from her family. Having to guide her littlest sister through this stressful situation was challenging from so far away, but soon an ambulance was on the way to take their mom to the hospital.

At the hospital, they concluded she had suffered a seizure, so they ordered scans. The MRI indicated a giant mass in her brain. Bre's younger siblings were terrified, and so was she. Bre called her husband and asked him to come home from work. They packed all their kids in the car so that they could drive to be with her mom and family. She tried to keep herself together and be strong since she was the oldest sibling, but deep down inside she felt like she was a little girl falling apart too.

The doctors ended up taking Bre's mom to surgery to try to remove the tumor in her brain. As Bre sat in the surgical waiting room with her father and siblings, anxiety lingered. A few hours into the surgery, a phone call came through saying the procedure was going to take longer than the doctors anticipated because they wanted to make sure they got everything. This news got everyone's hopes up, so when the doctors finished the surgery and came to meet them in the waiting room, the family was not prepared for the news they were about to hear. The doctors said that unfortunately Bre's mom had stage four cancer and would have only a few more months to live. Bre fell to her knees in agony and pain. The family was completely devastated beyond what any words could express by this shocking news.

Bre was very close to her mom. She was a comfort to Bre, so imagining life without her felt impossible—especially since her mother was so young. Bre grew up believing in and having a relationship with Jesus, but walking through this situation caused her to question where God was. It felt like God had left her family. She was wrestling with so many feelings of doubt, and she desperately needed help to make it through the grief she was experiencing. Not only did Bre have four younger siblings to comfort, but she also had her own five-year-old twins and a three-year-old. She questioned how she could care for and feed her own children when she was barely able to take care of herself.

Bre's dad was a pastor at a big church, so many people came to surround them as they were walking through this deep pain. But rather than sitting with them in their grief and pain, a lot of the people tried to give their best advice or share a Bible verse. Those aren't necessarily bad things, but when you are experiencing deep grief, you need a listening ear and an empathetic heart, not a lecture or words that try to mask the pain and intense heaviness of the trial.

As Bre began to navigate this new situation with her entire family, she knew she needed to cling to Jesus in a way she had never done before, but it felt nearly impossible. She had to remind herself, *I don't choose to trust God because things in my life are going to be good; I can trust Him solely because He is good.*

One night Bre was unable to hold back the tears streaming down her face. Not only was she grieving the fact that she was losing her mom, but she was also in agony over what it meant for so many other people. She didn't know what to do except open her Bible. She came across Psalm 91 where it says, "Whoever dwells in the shelter of the Most High will rest in the shadow of the Almighty. I will say of the LORD, 'He is my refuge and my fortress, my God, in whom I trust.'"[1] Instead of feeling close to God as she continued to read, she felt so far from Him—as if these words were not true. Through this grief, she was learning that God doesn't *always* save us from pain, but He is *always* with us in it.

> "Whoever dwells in the shelter of the Most High
>
> will rest in the shadow of the Almighty."

Bre began to picture herself as a little girl stepping into her mom's shadow. As she sat with Psalm 91 and this mental picture, she felt as if the Lord was showing her what it meant to rest in *His* shadow. She wasn't seeing God in full at the moment, but she was in His shadow. She wasn't in heaven with Him, but as she pictured herself stepping into His shadow, her own shadow disappeared—and she realized that she was dwelling with Him. As she began to picture God dwelling with her, verses that she had known and memorized as a little girl began to take root in her heart and flood her mind. These words from God gave her life at a time when she felt like she couldn't breathe. She was learning that the promises of God were true in her pain, and she was choosing to trust in His character.

Through her grief, my mother-in-law began to shift from a worldly to an eternal perspective. She realized that we cannot put our hope in trying to achieve the Christian American dream, but rather we must place our hope in what we cannot see, the One who is everlasting.

We know the waters are going to get rough and rocky. We are going to have trials. We are going to experience grief. The darkness of the world is real. And when those things come our way, what are we going to hold on to? My mother-in-law made the choice to stand on God's promises through this hard season with her mother, as well as other trials that came later in her life. She firmly stood on Isaiah 43:

But now thus says the LORD,
he who created you, O Jacob,
    he who formed you, O Israel:
"Fear not, for I have redeemed you;
    I have called you by name, you are mine.
When you pass through the waters, I will be with you;
    and through the rivers, they shall not overwhelm you;
when you walk through fire you shall not be burned,
    and the flame shall not consume you.
For I am the LORD your God,
    the Holy One of Israel, your Savior."
    (verses 1–3, ESV)

From that phone call with her little sister to nine months later when her mom passed away, Bre clung to the words in these verses and the true fact that God was her savior through it all. She had a new hunger for heaven. Her heart began to shift and see that heaven would, in fact, be a better place for her mom. And when Bre was in the room with her mom when she went to be with Jesus, she felt closer to God than she ever had before.

I tell you this story of my mother-in-law because grief, tragedy, and unexpected hardships are going to happen in our lives—or maybe already have happened in your life. And that dark place is where the Enemy wants you to stay. That is where Satan targets us and makes us doubt everything we may know about God. The feelings are so raw, so real, and so hard to navigate. The darkness feels all-consuming, and it seems impossible to see even a sliver of light in the situation. But when we feel like we are in a boat in a storm, when we feel like the waters are raging with no end in sight, we have a Lighthouse we can fix our gaze on.

I recently read that "lighthouses have traditionally been viewed as symbols of hope and security. As beacons of light, they provide guidance for safe passage to sailors and protect not only their lives but the land nearby."[2] Jesus is our firm hope and security as He guides us through the rough waters and stays with us in them. And not only do we have Jesus to guide us and be with us through the hardest of the hard times, we also have His Word to stand firm on. My mother-in-law also stood on Psalm 119:105, "Your word is a lamp for my feet, a light on my path." She chose to put her hope in these words even when she didn't understand her circumstances. She told me, "Not only was the Word my lighthouse, but the Holy Spirit also brought the words to life for me." She didn't feel like she was just reading some words in the Bible; they seemed so real and personal to her. She experienced that by God's power and goodness. And it is by His power and goodness that you are able to fully experience His comfort in your own life as well.

My mother-in-law made it through that season of her life with victory. When the waters truly did feel like they had overtaken her, she didn't let them define her. She let God's truth define her. She made space for God's Word to be alive and active in her life. To be honest with you, I don't believe in the saying, "God will never give you more than you can handle." I believe that on our own we cannot handle most things. God wants our dependency. He wants to work in our lives. Sometimes we are given more than we can handle on our own, but in Christ's power, we will always be victorious.

WILL I MAKE IT THROUGH THESE ROUGH WATERS?

The story in Acts 27 and 28 deeply encourages my heart. We see in Acts 27 that the apostle Paul was a prisoner for proclaiming God's Word. He, along with some other prisoners, was put on a ship sailing to Rome. The Lord had promised Paul that he would go to Rome to appeal before Caesar, and this promise was about to be fulfilled. But the journey there was far from easy. The wind was against them, and they were struggling to sail. Paul spoke up to the officials about how bad the weather was for their safety, saying, "I believe there is trouble ahead if we go on—shipwreck, loss of cargo, and danger to our lives as well."[3] The officials disregarded Paul's comment, and the captain continued onward.

As they pressed on, the weather changed abruptly and winds the strength of a typhoon came and pushed them far out into the sea. The storm was so bad that those on the ship began to throw cargo into the water. The weather lasted for many days and nights. Since they had not eaten for a long time, Paul spoke to the men, saying:

Men, you should have listened to me in the first place and not left Crete. You would have avoided all this damage and loss. But take courage! None of you will lose your lives, even though the ship will go down. For last night an angel of the God to whom I belong and whom I serve stood beside me, and he said, "Don't be afraid, Paul, for you will surely stand trial before Caesar! What's more, God in his goodness has granted safety to everyone sailing with you." So take courage! For I believe God. It will be just as he said. But we will be shipwrecked on an island. (Acts 27:21–26, NLT)

Take a minute to picture this scene. Try to put yourself in Paul's shoes and imagine how he was feeling. First, simply for preaching God's Word, Paul was in prison, which had to have been difficult. Then he was put on this ship with other prisoners, most of whom were actual criminals. And now they are going through this storm that probably should have caused the ship to sink! The Lord told Paul, "Don't be afraid." Even though Paul was on a boat during a wild storm, he chose to stand firm on the word that the Lord told him. Can you imagine *not* being afraid during this?

Once Paul said those words we read in verses 21–26, the sailors began to get scared and tried to jump ship, but Paul told the soldiers, "You will all die unless the sailors stay aboard."[4] So the soldiers decided to cut the ropes of the life boats. Paul then urged everyone to eat; they all hadn't eaten in almost two weeks because of the continual storm. Paul broke bread with everyone on the ship. The next day they began to see a coastline, but they were unsure which coastline it was. And just like the Lord told Paul, the ship hit a shoal, which ran the ship aground on an island. Everyone had to jump off the ship—those who couldn't swim held on to broken planks or debris—and all made it safely ashore.

As he was literally in a storm that should have overtaken them, notice what Paul clung to: God's word. Paul was not afraid because God said that he didn't need to be afraid and that he would eventually make it to Rome. Paul chose to stand on the truth and character of God through some of the most challenging weeks of his life. Paul clung to those words, and God was faithful to fulfill His promises. Everyone—prisoners, soldiers, and sailors—made it safely to shore.

God isn't wasting your story.

The story continues in Acts 28, where they learned they were on Malta. The people who lived on the island of Malta made a fire for Paul, the prisoners, and the shipmen and provided food and water for them. As Paul was collecting firewood, a poisonous snake bit his hand, a bite that could have easily killed him. But because of God's call on his life, miraculously, he was not harmed. The people on the island thought that he must be a god, but little did they know that it was the power of God within him that protected him.

The father of the chief official of the island was very ill at this time. Paul prayed over him, and he was healed. Because Paul healed this man, every other person on the island who was sick came to be healed by Paul. Then the people of the island showered Paul and everyone who had been shipwrecked with him with honor and supplied everything they needed to sail to Rome.[5]

If the storm had never happened, Paul would not have ended up on Malta. God knew there were people there who needed to be healed on Malta. And while the storm had to have been incredibly terrifying, God was faithful to get them through safely. Because of that storm, God was able to do what only He can do. Not only did God fulfill His promise to get them safely to shore, but He supernaturally provided a way for them to make it to Rome. Paul's hope wasn't in the ship that was taking him where he wanted to go; his hope was in God who would take him where he needed to go.

When we go through storms that seem like they are going to sink us, we have to remember that our hope can't be in "the ship." If we place our hope in temporary things, we will end up shipwrecked. But when our hope is in Jesus, it cannot be overcome or shaken. Hebrews 6:19 says, "This hope is a strong and trustworthy anchor for our souls. It leads us through the curtain into God's inner sanctuary" (NLT). When our hope is in the One who is eternal rather than in what is temporal, we will make it through every storm without being completely overcome. The One who overcame keeps us from being overcome by the world. The Light that came keeps us from being overcome by darkness.

I heard Christine Caine teach on this passage once, and she talked about how some of us are on Malta right now. We thought we would be in our Rome, but for whatever reason, storms, rocky waters, and unexpected things have happened, and we aren't quite where we thought we would be. But look at what took place with Paul—who never expected to be on the island of Malta. The Bible never says that Paul was upset about not being in Rome. After what took place in Malta, I imagine that Paul recognized the reason and need of the detour. Many miracles took place because Paul had an open heart to what God wanted to do in and through him while he was on Malta.

Maybe for you the storms have taken you to places you never thought you would be. But what if there are miracles that could happen right in front of you if you shift your focus away from where you want to go and on to where God has you? Maybe God will take you to that place you want to go, or maybe He has a different story for you. Whatever it may be, God isn't wasting your story. He has a purpose for you right where you are. Lean into Him and what He may want to teach you. Know that when you stand firm in His truth, you cannot be shaken.

GOD IS OUR GUIDING LIGHT

When the waters got rough for my mother-in-law and when the waves literally got rough for Paul, they navigated them very similarly: by standing on God's truth. Jesus, too, stood on the truth of God when times got tough. We see this in Matthew 4, when Jesus was in the desert being tempted by Satan. Let's look at exactly how Jesus stood against the temptations of the Enemy:

Then Jesus was led by the Spirit into the wilderness to be tempted by the devil. After fasting forty days and forty nights, he was hungry. The tempter came to him and said, "If you are the Son of God, tell these stones to become bread."

Jesus answered, "It is written: 'Man shall not live on bread alone, but on every word that comes from the mouth of God.'"

Then the devil took him to the holy city and had him stand on the highest point of the temple. "If you are the Son of God," he said, "throw yourself down. For it is written:

"'He will command his angels concerning you,
     and they will lift you up in their hands,
          so that you will not strike your foot against a stone.'"

Jesus answered him, "It is also written: 'Do not put the Lord your God to the test.'"

Again, the devil took him to a very high mountain and showed him all the kingdoms of the world and their splendor. "All this I will give you," he said, "if you will bow down and worship me."

Jesus said to him, "Away from me, Satan! For it is written: 'Worship the Lord your God, and serve him only.'" (Matthew 4:1–10)

Not only did Jesus live His life using God's truth to get Him through challenging times, but He also said, "Man shall not live on bread alone, but on every word that comes from the mouth of God" (Matthew 4:4).

When it feels like our own circumstances are too much to bear, when the raging sea feels like it is going to sink us, the one thing we can count on to guide us through as our lighthouse is the active Word of God. His Word is a lamp for us. His Word is the light that we and this world need, and we have full access to it. My mother in-law can attest to the power of God's Word. It just takes us making the choice to elevate the voice of God over the voice of the noisy and loud world.

Elevate the voice of God over the voice

of the noisy and loud world.

There are many verses in the Bible we can refer to that will help us pray when it seems too hard to muster up the words on our own. Some of my favorite verses for asking God to help when things feel impossible come from Psalm 119. When the waters around you are rocky and life begins to feel like too much to bear, say a simple prayer: *Jesus, help me.* Lay all your feelings, thoughts, and worries at His feet. Read Psalm 119. Reach out to a friend. Make the choice to let God's Word be your lighthouse when you feel lost out in the scary sea. He is with you. He will guide you. He has never left you nor will He ever leave you.

As you live your life doing your best to shine His light, remember that His light is always shining right at you through His guiding Word.

Teach me, LORD, the way of your decrees,
    that I may follow it to the end.
Give me understanding, so that I may keep your law
    and obey it with all my heart.
Direct me in the path of your commands,
    for there I find delight.
Turn my heart toward your statutes
    and not toward selfish gain.
Turn my eyes away from worthless things;
    preserve my life according to your word.
Fulfill your promise to your servant,
    so that you may be feared.
Take away the disgrace I dread,
    for your laws are good.
How I long for your precepts!
    In your righteousness preserve my life.
    (Psalm 119:33–40)

ARISE AND SHINE

- Read all of Psalm 119.
- Look back on your life in times when you have been in a storm. How was God your lighthouse then?
- Pick one verse that means a lot to you and memorize it. When you are in a storm, let these be the words you meditate on. Let this be the light that guides you.

10

PROTECTING YOUR LIGHT

Where and How We Can Place
Boundaries in Our Lives

*They always comment on her photos and not mine because they
like her more.*
I'm losing followers, and it's a reflection of who I am.
I will never get to where she is.
*They all hung out and didn't invite me because they think I'm
annoying.*
*My words aren't as important or powerful as theirs, so I should
just not share them.*

THESE WERE REAL THOUGHTS and feelings I was struggling
with in March of 2021. I had lost sight of why I was doing what
I do on social media. I was comparing myself to others and letting those thoughts define who I was. I thought that having a
following would bring more credibility to what I was doing. I
saw all of these other people with followings, and it seemed like
their lives were put together and they had all of the friends in the
world. And that is what I thought I wanted. I mean isn't that
what we all want? To be deeply known and loved?

I now know that I was falling into the lies of the Enemy, secretly believing them, and really struggling with them. I had no boundaries for the amount of time I was spending on social media, and it was taking a toll. My mind was consumed with images and stories of things that I was trying to attain for myself. Rather than speaking God's truth over myself, I was looking to others to help fill the void deep in my heart. My eyes were fixed more on the words of others than on the words of the Lord.

Social media *can* be good—don't get me wrong. But if we don't create boundaries, it will end up consuming us and affecting us more than we realize. When we are constantly bombarding our brains with videos of what other people's houses look like, how they spend their time, where they put their money, what they say you should buy, and who they think is important, it is going to impact us. We may say it doesn't affect us, but when we look at something, it finds a spot in our brains. And then when we are on social media for multiple hours each day, those influences begin to take up even more brain space than we recognize.

As of 2022, the average amount of time worldwide that a person spends per day on social media is 147 minutes.[1] That's almost two and a half hours. And the time spent by teens was much higher. A study done from 2019 to 2022 showed that teens spent up to eight hours on social media per day.[2]

When we are on social media, we see what others are up to, which leads us to compare our lives to theirs. And that can lead us to think too highly of ourselves or leave us feeling lonely and depressed. There is also now so much more room for bullying through social media, not only in younger generations but in every generation. Social media has created a space for people to hide behind a screen and say words that they would probably never say in person. As you can see, without strict boundaries, it can be really tough in the social media world.

I didn't realize I had an unhealthy relationship with social media until my husband pointed it out to me. Then I knew I needed to make a change in my life. About that time, I was sitting at my kitchen table with some girlfriends. We were catching up and having raw conversations about where we were in our lives. One of my friends (actually, Darsha, from chapter 5) said she had just started to do a challenge in which she would wear only a select few pieces of clothing, do the Whole30 diet program, and delete social media for thirty days. She was only a few days in, but she said she was already feeling so much peace and was more aware of what God was doing in her life. As soon as she began talking about giving up her social media, my heart started racing, my palms began sweating, and I knew that the Lord was trying to tell me something.

The next morning, as I started doing my quiet time with the Lord, I felt Him tugging on my heart to give up social media for a period. During this time my Instagram had been growing fast, and I liked it. I was afraid that if I gave it up for a while, I would lose followers and not achieve any of the goals I had set. Clearly, the Enemy was trying so hard to get me to give in to the desires of my flesh. Yet, I felt the Lord's conviction tenderly tell me, *How could you think you could do anything for yourself on social media better than what I could do with you off of it?*

Tears began to stream down my cheeks as I realized how much pressure I had been putting on myself by trying to find my worth through social media. My eyes were opened to what was going on and I realized I had been believing lies that the Enemy had spoken over me. I felt a sense of freedom as I sat with the words the Lord sweetly told me. I thought, *How could I ever think I could*

do anything better in my own strength than the Lord could do for me?
I asked God how long I should take a break from it and felt Him
say forty days. *Are You sure, Lord? Did I hear You right?* In that
moment, I deleted social media from my phone.

Friend, those forty days were some of the best of my life because that is when I deeply, sincerely, and wholeheartedly fell in
love with the Word of God. Without taking those forty days off,
I don't think I would be where I am today. In fact, I probably
wouldn't have written this book. God did supernatural and beautiful work in my heart in those days when I was no longer filling
my mind with what I thought I needed. Looking back, it was
simple; I just needed Jesus. Now, I am forever thankful for the
strength the Lord imparted to me to take that break. Since then,
my relationship with social media has completely changed, and I
am now able to recognize for myself when it's beginning to get
unhealthy. But just in case, I also asked my husband to speak up
when he feels a break is needed.

I have learned that God sometimes asks us to say no to things—
even good things—because He has something better in mind.
Often, we want to discern for ourselves what is best for us. But in
everything, we should go to the Lord first and foremost for guidance and direction. It can be scary to do that, especially when we
are afraid we won't be able to do what we want. But He can do
immeasurably more than we could ever ask or even think of on
our own![3]

A prayer I now pray often is:

*Lord, help me to discern what is a holy yes and what is a holy no.
You know where I am to go; help me get there in Your timing.
Give me supernatural patience and strength to say yes to the
right things and no to the wrong things. Help me to guard my
heart so that what flows from it is glorifying to You. Amen.*

This prayer isn't just for big decisions in my life. It's also for the little ones like what to watch on TV, what movies to see, whom I choose to spend a lot of time with, what kind of music I listen to, and, of course, how much time I spend on social media.

God sometimes asks us to say no to things—even good things—because He has something better in mind.

Maybe it isn't social media that you need to take a break from—or maybe it is. Just know that what we consume through media, what we do with our time, and who we hang out with *matters*. If we don't set guardrails for ourselves, we can end up feeling depressed, anxious, or overwhelmed. The darkness can feel all-consuming. But we can choose to limit our exposure to the darkness of the world. And while we cannot control it all, we can control some of it—before it controls us.

When it comes to being a light for Christ, there will be times we need to say no to things to protect ourselves. Like it says in Proverbs 4:23, "Above all else, guard your heart, for everything you do flows from it."

PUT THE RAILS UP

In the Bible we are told multiple times that we should guard our hearts and our minds from things that are of the flesh. Ephesians 5:10–11 says, "Carefully determine what pleases the Lord. Take no part in the worthless deeds of evil and darkness; instead, expose them" (NLT).

I am definitely not perfect at this. There are times when I mess up and end up watching something that wasn't the best for me. So, as I give you the advice below, know that I am working at it alongside you. This is something that no human is perfect at, so have grace over yourself. What I pray is that your mind would be opened to the truth that everything we consume affects us.

I want to share ways that I try to guard my heart from some of the most common influences that you are probably exposed to as well.

SOCIAL MEDIA

Once I went back on social media after my forty-day fast, I knew I needed to implement some type of boundary with it, otherwise I would set a time limit on my social media apps and just end up pressing "add fifteen more minutes" over and over again. My brother-in-law taught me the best way to help with social media time limits—at least with iPhones. (You might have to figure out another method for other devices.) You can set a passcode for the time limit for the specific apps. For example, for Facebook, Instagram, and TikTok I allow myself only an hour and twenty minutes per day for all three. Once the time limit hits, the apps close. To add more time, you have to enter the passcode. My brother-in-law gave me this tip: Have someone else create the passcode. My husband set my passcode, so he's the only one who can add time to my limit. If you want to try this but aren't married, have a parent or best friend set it for you. Doing this trick has helped me to intentionally limit the time that I spend scrolling and consuming. I've told some of my friends about this little life hack, and it has really helped them too!

Being intentional in setting my time limit has helped my mindset way more than I expected it to. I have been doing it now for a few years and have noticed a huge difference in my relation-ship with social media. Of course, there are times when I ask my husband to add time to it if I am working and have to be on so-cial media more, but I do really try to stick to it. I understand that everyone doesn't struggle with social media to the extent that I do, but I wish I would have learned this a long time ago to protect myself from the way it has negatively affected me.

Another guardrail to put up when it comes to social media is to take more control of what you allow yourself to see. Who are you following? Who can you unfollow? Is there someone you follow who posts sexual photos or is always complaining or talks down about other people? Do you find you're constantly com-paring yourself to a particular person you follow? If what they are posting is taking more away from your joy than adding to it, there is no reason for you to follow them. Or if their posts are causing you to fall into sin, then that is 100 percent a reason to unfollow them. If they are a good friend of yours and you don't want to unfollow them, you can just skip over their posts or "hide" them. If what they're doing is harmful, consider having a conversation with them. But remember, you can't control what other people post—only what you consume and how you react. Ask the Lord for holy discernment about whom you are follow-ing and what you are seeing on social media.

VISUAL ENTERTAINMENT

Just because a new movie came out and everyone is watching it doesn't mean that you have to. This is something else I have per-sonally wrestled with. I want to keep up with the trends and stay in "the know." And that led me to view things that I am not proud of watching. When it comes to entertainment, we often care about what our kids watch, but we seem to take away all boundaries when it comes to ourselves. We often give a pass to things like offensive language, violence, and sexual or graphic content. Again, we may not think it affects us, but it truly does.

The way we see other people interact with one another on a TV show or movie can seep into how we interact with others. We create expectations for how we want things to play out in real life according to what we have seen. In many cases, it's just not healthy.

Sometimes we even make time to watch TV before we spend time with other people. It's so easy to get hooked on favorite shows, and often it seems like our lives are under the control of the screen in front of us.

I am not saying that you have to stop watching movies or TV. I simply want you to become aware of how much it could be affecting your life. When you watch something, ask yourself, *Does my television consumption rule my free time? Am I proud of myself for watching this? Would I be okay if my child saw this? Would I watch this if Jesus was sitting in person with me?*

What are some changes you may need to make to what you watch? If there is a lot of sexual content in what you watch, you may find that is something you come to desire more and more. Not only that, but it could create an unhealthy and false reality of what sex should look like. What about violence? Is it beneficial for you to watch violent programming? Does it cause you to have anxiety or nightmares? What about profanity? Has it negatively impacted the way you speak?

I remember when I was in middle school, my friends and I would watch a show called *That's So Raven*. A favorite phrase of the main character was "Oh, snap!" So my friends and I would also say it as a reaction to something shocking or as a replacement for "Darn it!" And we only said it because we continually heard it on this show. And while a simple saying like "Oh, snap!" is innocuous, my point is that it's easy to incorporate a particular phrase into our everyday conversation simply from hearing it repeatedly. There are many other expressions we hear in shows that are not clean, and we can easily begin to say them as well. And what is the benefit of it? To make ourselves feel good? To sound cool? Truly, why do we feel the need to use these words? Well, when we are constantly filling our minds with these words through entertainment or who we hang out with, it begins to feel more acceptable to say them. It becomes a habit for us, and then it can become hard to stop.

I want us to think about the why behind what we watch, how it affects us, and most importantly how it affects others seeing Jesus in us.

Our Community

Finally, let's talk about the area that is one of the most important but can also be the hardest when it comes to creating boundaries: the people we hang out with. Whether or not we want to believe it, "We become who we hang out with."[4]

To start, I want you to take time to examine your life right now. Are you proud of who you are? Of what you are doing? Of the things you do in the hidden and secret place when no one watches? Are you proud of the way you speak? The way you treat others? The way you treat yourself? Interestingly, a lot of our answers to these questions are impacted by those whom we spend the most time with.

When the answer to those questions is no, or "I'm working on it," it's important that the people we hang out with the most are willing to support us through the process of making a positive shift. If your community doesn't want what is best for you or isn't trying to help you grow in a healthy direction, I highly recommend evaluating your friendships. After all, we were made to be in community. And not just a community that we see occasionally but deep and intentional community. We truly need one another. Remember, Jesus didn't do life alone. He had His close friends with whom He shared life—friends who knew what He was going through, who knew what He was learning, who prayed with Him, and who walked with Him through hard times.

Our walk with Jesus isn't supposed to be easy or comfortable;

it is to be a life lived against the grain of this world.

Who are your people? And are you proud that they are your people? Do you admire the way they live? Do they call you higher as a person? Do they make you want to be closer to Jesus? These are very important questions to ask.

For so long in my life, I just wanted to be friends with the people who seemed to have it all together—you know, those that I thought had "made it." Very quickly I realized that a lot of my friendships with these people were superficial. My husband's friendships were completely different. He always says he would "rather have a very few friendships that are a mile deep than a mile-long line of friendships that are just an inch deep." It's very important that we go deep with the people we surround ourselves with, since they are the ones we trust with the hardest of the hard. So, when it comes to deciding who those people are, it is okay to be picky and not let just anyone pour into you.

We are influenced by who and what we are surrounded by. If your group of friends is always wanting to cause trouble, getting drunk multiple nights a week, or pushing you to do things you feel uncomfortable doing, then that is going to influence you. If they are always gossiping, talking down to people, and using foul language, odds are, eventually you may start speaking that way without even realizing it. And I am not saying you can't hang out with people who do these things. Obviously, we must love the lost and broken, as we, too, are broken. It's when those people are our primary friends that their habits begin to rub off on us. And I'm not trying to shame anyone but rather make you aware of the importance of community.

You can hang out with all the people you want. You can be friends with a lot of people. But make sure you have those few friendships that go a mile deep. And for the ones that go a mile deep, make sure they are people you admire, trust, and who push you to be the best version of yourself. When you find these friends, protect them. Make space and room for them in your life. Let the walls down and let people see you for who you are and who God has made you to be.

LIVE AS THOSE WHO ARE WISE

When it comes to setting boundaries in our lives, a lot of times the Enemy tries to discourage us by making us feel like we are missing out. He does a good job at making worldly things seem very appealing—sometimes more appealing than eternal life with Jesus. And although a life walking with Jesus may be a life of fewer worldly things, it means a life of more eternal things. Our walk with Jesus isn't supposed to be easy or comfortable; it is to be a life lived against the grain of this world. Ephesians 5:15–17 says, "So be careful how you live. Don't live like fools, but like those who are wise. Make the most of every opportunity in these evil days. Don't act thoughtlessly, but understand what the Lord wants you to do" (NLT).

The Light of the world lives in us, so it is important to care about how what we do, see, and hear impacts us. While setting boundaries and making changes can be difficult, it is completely possible with the help of the Holy Spirit. My friend, your calling is to be a child of light. As much as the things of this world feel promising and fulfilling, there is nothing more promising or more fulfilling than the hope of Jesus. Ask the Lord to help show you the areas in your life that need to be protected. Take baby steps toward the abundance that He has for you, even though that may mean saying no to what seem to be good things. God knows what is best for you. And sometimes His best for you means setting boundaries in certain areas of your life in order to let His light shine brightly through you.

ARISE AND SHINE

- In what area do you struggle with having boundaries?
- What is something you can do today to set a boundary?
- I challenge you to take a few days off from social media. Spend time with the Lord and make space to hear from Him.

PART III

SHINING LIGHT

You are the light of the world. A city set on a hill cannot be hidden. Nor do people light a lamp and put it under a basket, but on a stand, and it gives light to all in the house.

—MATTHEW 5:14–15, ESV

11

FAN THE FLAME

Finding Fresh Wind When Your Light Feels Dimmed

WHEN I WAS IN college, I wasn't as aware of my desperate need for the Lord as I am now. It was a season of smooth sailing. I felt like I was on top of the world. Friendships were healthy, grades were where I wanted them to be, I was being invited to fun and exciting gatherings, and I was stoked on life. When things were good, I honestly would forget my need for the Lord.

Other seasons were much harder. Sometimes I felt completely alone, unwanted or unseen, and I would sink down deep into dark feelings. During these times, I would question: *Am I enough? Do people care about me? Do I add much value to this world?* When things were bad, I was more attuned to the Lord and I begged Him to change my circumstances.

To be honest, I think that is how a lot of us can be at times. When life is going well according to our terms, we lose sight of our continual and desperate need for the Lord. Then, when we hit rock bottom or when life heads in a direction we don't want it to go, we wonder where God is. We question what He is doing, and we beg and plead for Him to help us and change our circumstances. But He is worthy of our continued attention and desperation, no matter our situation. Our dependence on Him should never change, even if our circumstances do.

When it comes to being a bright light for Christ, we must be on the lookout for two things: becoming complacent and becoming comparative. Complacency and comparison are where the Enemy loves to sit and lie to us. Let's dive into these words, see what they mean, look at seasons that I and my friends have been through, and explore how we navigated our way through them in victory with the Lord.

FIGHTING COMPLACENCY

Because we are fallen and sinful humans, it is nearly impossible to be on fire for Jesus 100 percent of every second of every day for our entire lives. I am not saying it is fully impossible, but odds are you have had a season of complacency in your faith. And if you haven't yet, you may eventually. The definition of complacency is being self-satisfied.[1] Being complacent in our faith is when we choose to do life without depending on the Lord. In talking with others about complacency in our walks with Jesus, I've learned that it usually stems from two things. The first is what I mentioned above: the feeling that we don't need Jesus because things are going well. And the second is the fear that God isn't going to answer our prayers or show up the way we want Him to, so we shrink back and don't engage as much with Him as we should.

I talked with one of my friends, Krista, about a season of complacency that she recently walked through. She runs a ministry called Live Salted that equips women who are following Jesus to disciple and lead across generations. She's held many women's conferences from Seattle to California and all the way to New Zealand. She is a dear friend whom I admire; she has helped me grow personally in my faith and hunger for the Lord.

We talked about how complacency can stem from many different situations, and people who are at various stages in their faith can struggle with it. Complacency can look different for different people. That said, let me be clear that Krista's story describes what complacency looks like for *her,* based on what she has walked through and what she has done to fight against it.

Krista found herself in a season of complacency at the end of two large back-to-back conferences. She went from being around people constantly, hearing their stories, and seeing how God was moving . . . to suddenly not being around people. That gave room for the Enemy to come in and tell her that God wasn't at work. She found herself not pursuing the Lord like she had in previous seasons of her life. In addition to that, God had called her to take some steps back and rebuild part of the foundation of her ministry. That meant she had a lot of administrative and data work to do, which she found to be lonely, exhausting, and defeating. Looking back, she also realized how much not being plugged into a deep, Christ-centered community affected her personal walk with the Lord.

After a few months of struggle, Krista had to jump into a season of fundraising since Live Salted is a nonprofit. There were times it was hard to trust that the Lord would answer her prayers for what they needed financially when the money was not coming in like they had hoped. Because she was not seeing how the Lord was actively at work in her own life in that season, she ended up trying to do a lot of things in her own way and with her own strength—without God. Can you relate? (I know I am raising my hand over here.)

It's important to realize that being in those seasons is not what

God has for us nor is it where He wants us to stay. So, in order to get out of a season of complacency, we must actively do something. It's not just going to magically go away. We must take a step toward God to take a baby step away from being complacent. Once one step is taken, it becomes easier to take another, then another, and so on till we are in the next season.

As we continued to chat about this time of her life, I asked Krista what she did to help herself get out of it. One of the things she did was listen to the testimonies of others. Krista would listen to stories on the I Am Second website or call a friend and ask what God was doing in her life. For Krista, and probably for most of us, it is so encouraging to hear how God is at work in the lives of others. It reminds us that if God did it for them, He can do it for us. And here's something to keep in mind: Other people's faith increases when they hear the testimony of what God is doing or has done in *your* life. So remember that your story matters and has more kingdom impact than you will ever know. It's not up to us to control the impact of our stories but rather to be good stewards of them.

He is always working on our behalf for His glory.

If you are in a season of complacency with your faith right now, I want to encourage you that God sees you where you are, but He doesn't want you to stay there. He truly has so much more for you than you could ever ask or imagine. My prayer for you today is that you would take one tiny bold step forward. Whether that is telling someone about the season you are in so they can join you in prayer, asking someone about what God is doing in their life, reading a book, or listening to a podcast that may encourage you.

I want to speak the truth over you that God is at work in your life, even if you can't feel it. He is always working on our behalf for His glory. I also want to say I am so sorry if this season has been hard, because I know that it can feel defeating and lonely. Know that you are 100 percent not alone nor will you ever be. Don't let the lies of the Enemy keep you where he wants you. Stomp on his lies with the truth of the Lord and take baby steps out of this season and into the next.

If you haven't been in a season of complacency recently, I hope and pray that you remember this chapter when you find yourself there in the future. Our faith will ebb and flow because we are humans in a spiritual war, but in Jesus you are victorious. So, if a season of struggling to be on fire for Christ comes your way, come back to this chapter and be reminded that you aren't alone and that there is always so much more for you than you could ever possibly imagine.

Complacency is often a feeling of being unmotivated. That burning fire within our souls to know Jesus more just isn't quite there like it was before. So, how can we go from being unmotivated to motivated? It all comes down to where our hearts are and what is going on in them. Some questions to ask yourself are:

1. *Where are these feelings of being unmotivated in my faith coming from? Did something happen to me? Did I see something? Did I experience something? When did it start?*
2. *What is causing me to not do anything about it? Do I feel stuck in this spot for any particular reason?*
3. *What is one step I can take today toward Jesus? What is one thing I can do today that may be hard but will pay off in the long run?*

These questions can help us understand where we are and why we are feeling the way we do. I think a lot of times we rush through life and forget to do heart check-ins. I get that it can be really hard when it feels like you are putting work in but aren't seeing any fruit right away. Know that any step toward the Lord never goes unnoticed. And hold on to the truth that He is with you in every season, whether you feel it or not. One step at a time, my friend. You will make it through.

An image that the Lord has placed on my heart about complacency and the light of Christ within us is a burning fire. Imagine yourself standing in front of a campfire, flannel shirt on, coffee in hand, watching it burn brightly. Picture yourself and your faith as the burning fire. Occasionally little embers fly off from the fire. When we become complacent, our faith turns into a flying ember. There is endless possibility and potential for that little ember to become an even bigger fire, but it needs a fresh wind. When that wind comes and takes that ember to proper ground, it becomes another bright and burning fire. It will not come magically (as we would hope); instead, we must choose to draw near to the One who will give us fresh wind.

KICKING COMPARISON

Alright, y'all. Time to talk in more detail about one thing that is so hard to admit to doing. The thing that the Enemy uses to make us feel like we will never be good enough: *comparing ourselves to others.* I am going to be honest with you. Originally, I wasn't going to put this section in the book. After all, I had mentioned it in previous chapters, like where we talked about the downside of social media. *Wasn't that sufficient?* It wasn't until I was writing this chapter that I caught myself comparing myself to other authors and then felt inadequate to write the book and wanted to give up. As I navigated those feelings and talked through them with my husband, I realized that this topic needs to be addressed in more detail when it comes to being a light for Christ. Comparing ourselves to others is something we all have done and may do again, so it is important that we equip ourselves and know how to overcome it!

Thoughts I have had before and hate to admit are:

If only I had what she had, then I would be happier.
I wish I was that loved. It looks like everyone loves her so much.
It looks like that is working out for her really well. Why does
   nothing ever work out like that for me?
They always like, comment on, and share her photos. They must
   like her more than me.
Wow, she has got it all together all the time, and I just feel like a
   mess all the time.
Everyone is going to think more highly of her than me because she
   is more known.

Oof.

I am not proud of these thoughts in any way. But at some point in my life, I thought each of them, and they consumed my mind and took away my joy. I share this with you because odds are you have also thought at least one of them, so I want you to know that you are not alone. I'm sure we've all had a twinge of jealousy at times like these: When she gets what you wanted. When he gets the job instead of you. When she gets what you feel like you've been waiting for your whole life. When it seems like the stars are aligning perfectly for him and all you want is for two stars to align for you.

I'm sure you've heard it said, "Comparison is the thief of joy." While that's true, I have come to realize that Satan is the real underlying thief of joy, and he does all that he can to try to make us believe that what we have isn't enough.

God is not only at work in our lives but also

in the lives of those around us.

Unfortunately, the hard truth is that comparison stems from the sin of pride. When we are focused on ourselves and what could benefit us, we lose sight of the fact that comparison causes fear because we're afraid that God won't do something for us that He has done for others, or we think that God doesn't love us as much. That mindset actually implies that God's power is limited—that He can help only this person and not us because there's not enough of Him to do both. But God is all-powerful! We need to let go of our pride and learn to celebrate what God is doing in the lives of others, not just our own lives.

Pride is a very sneaky sin, and it is one that no one likes to admit to. It also can be one that we don't realize has roots in our hearts—like a weed. If we let it take root, it begins to grow and damage anything around it. We need to rid ourselves of that weed.

To fight against pride, I recommend doing heart checks. Here are some questions that you can ask yourself if you notice that you are struggling with pride and comparison:

1. *Are there any thoughts in my heart today where I am the center?*
2. *Am I putting the needs of others first or my own?*

3. *In recent conversations, have I been trying to make myself
   known?*

While they can be hard questions to ask ourselves, especially
when the answers aren't what we wish they were, they are healthy
to ask. Once we remind ourselves that this life isn't about us but
instead is about the glory of God, our hearts get re-centered on
truth. Being centered on the truth of God and repenting of the
ways we have been prideful will kill the weeds of pride within our
hearts. We cannot overcome the struggle of comparison without
the One who has overcome it all.

It's so much easier said than done though, right? One minute
we are reading the Word of God and feel seen, known by Him,
and confident in our identity. Then the next minute we are scrolling on social media, filling our minds with content that makes us
feel like we are less than or that we need more. It is such a vicious
cycle and one that we have to fight with the strength of the Lord.

The words I stand on when I'm struggling with comparison
come from The Message paraphrase of 1 Corinthians 13:

Love never gives up.
Love cares more for others than for self.
Love doesn't want what it doesn't have.
Love doesn't strut,
Doesn't have a swelled head,
Doesn't force itself on others,
Isn't always "me first,"
Doesn't fly off the handle,
Doesn't keep score of the sins of others,
Doesn't revel when others grovel,
Takes pleasure in the flowering of truth,

Puts up with anything,
Trusts God always,
Always looks for the best,
Never looks back,
But keeps going to the end.
(verses 4–7)

Love doesn't want what it doesn't have and isn't always "me first."
On our own, we cannot love as 1 Corinthians instructs. But when
we rely on the strength of Christ, read and remind ourselves of
Scripture, and make Him the center of our hearts, His love begins to transform us to love like He does.

Ephesians is one of my favorite books of the Bible, and when
I am doubting where God has me, I always remind myself of this
verse: "For we are his workmanship, created in Christ Jesus for
good works, which God prepared beforehand, that we should
walk in them" (Ephesians 2:10, ESV). My friend, the plan for your
life that God has set before you is going to be different than His
plan for me or for anyone else. You can trust that God's perfect
plan will be more than you could have ever dreamed of or imagined for yourself. We live in a time where it can be so hard to see
and believe that because we have constant access through social
media to see what everyone else is up to. Our selfish and prideful
flesh begins to desire what the world defines as "making it." More
times than not, what our flesh desires doesn't line up with what
God desires for us. But in any given moment, it is so hard to remember, especially when we see someone else getting what we
desire.

Hold on to the truth that you are Christ's workmanship. You
are His masterpiece, created to do good works that were prepared for you before you were conceived in your mother's womb.

Ask the Lord to help you see what His desires are for your life and for His desires to become your heart's desires.

One thing I have discovered to help me overcome spurts of comparison is celebration. Romans 12:10 says, "Love each other with genuine affection, and take delight in honoring each other" (NLT). We are called to honor one another. We are called to celebrate one another! When we see and know that God is doing wondrous work in the life of a friend, it deserves celebration. But Satan is going to try to turn our focus to ourselves. He will trick us into thinking that God must not love us or care about us as much as our friend. Yet, God doesn't withhold anything good from those who walk uprightly with Him.[2] He is not withholding good from you just because you see good being done to someone else. So when God blesses another, may it become our goal to encourage, support, and celebrate, knowing full well that God is at work in that person's life! Let us be people who choose celebration over comparison.

Let us be people who choose celebration over comparison.

When we choose to take the focus off ourselves and put it onto others, a shift we can't stop takes place in our hearts. Jesus lived a life that focused on others and not Himself. Jesus celebrated others and put their needs before His. When we actively make the decision to live like Jesus, even when the decision is hard and goes against the grain of the world, we can't help but be transformed. You are fully capable of being someone who celebrates others when you rely on the strength of the Lord to help you.

Imagine a world where everyone chooses to celebrate what is going on in one another's lives. Now that would be a flame that could never be put out!

DON'T LET SATAN BLOW IT OUT

Complacency and comparison greatly impact the light we shine, and both originate from pride within our hearts. And, as we have seen, pride stems from being focused more on getting the glory for ourselves than for God. Sadie Robertson Huff gave a beautiful illustration of this during her talk at the 2023 Passion conference. She said, "[With] the iPhone, by design, you cannot be shining the light and looking at the camera at the same time. For some reason, by design, you cannot be shining the light and looking at yourself. For some reason, you cannot be trying to get the glory and give the glory."[3] You see, when we are wanting the glory, when we are wanting control, when we are wanting things to go exactly how we desire them to go, the focus of our hearts becomes ourselves. But we are not called to be split down the middle, serving ourselves and serving Jesus. We are called to live a life *fully* surrendered to Jesus. A life that undeniably points to Him and gives Him all of the glory rather than trying to receive some of the glory for ourselves.

We each have a spotlight within us. And guess what Satan wants? He wants you to focus on *you*! He knows that if you have your spotlight on yourself, then your light isn't going to point to Jesus. Do you want your spotlight to point to yourself? Or do you want it pointing to the glory of God?

Living in complacency and comparison is where the Enemy wants you to stay. He wants you to feel like there isn't more for you and that you aren't enough. But, my friend, the good news is that you are not meant to stay there. *You were not made to stay there!* You were made for so much more than you could ever ask or imagine. You were made to be set apart. You were made to share the good news of the Father. And you were made to live a life that shines the light of Christ, which then sparks the light of Christ within others. *That is your identity. That is where you are made and meant to be.* Not stuck in a place where the Enemy has a hold on you.

In and with the power of Jesus Christ, you have authority over those things.

In and with the power of Jesus Christ, you can declare that the Enemy will flee.

In and with the power of Jesus Christ, you can declare that your life is to be a spotlight to the glory of God and nothing else.

In and with the power of Jesus Christ, you can pray and ask for a fresh wind to come and set a fire for the Lord deep within your soul that you cannot contain.

ARISE AND SHINE

- Who can you choose to celebrate today? Send them a text, write them a letter, or get them a gift, and let them know that they mean a lot to you!
- If you are in a season of complacency, tell someone who isn't. Let them pour into you and encourage you in this season. Remember, one step forward at a time.

12

BE THE LIGHT

How to Live as the Hands and Feet of Jesus

HOSPITAL NURSES ARE TYPICALLY assigned a "home unit," an area in which they specialize and eventually become experts. I started out working with children who stayed the night or a few nights in the hospital after any type of surgery, but we also took care of short- and long-term rehabilitation patients on this unit. When I first started, I didn't know much. Fast-forward a few years, and now I feel very comfortable with this patient population. I have experienced a lot within this particular specialty, so I feel confident in caring for these sweet kids.

Occasionally as a nurse, you have to do what is called "floating." That means if another unit in the hospital is short-staffed and your unit is overstaffed, you "float" to that unit for a shift to help cover patient assignments. I am not exaggerating when I say this: Floating is a nurse's least favorite thing to do. It takes you out of your comfort zone and places you in an unfamiliar environment. You are on a unit that physically looks different than the one you are used to, so you don't know where any supplies are, you don't know the codes to the specific equipment rooms, and you truly feel like you're running around like a chicken with your head cut off. You also aren't with "your people." Since you don't know any of the other nurses, it can feel very isolating. On top of all that, you are assigned to patients you might not feel confident in caring for, since you're working outside your area of expertise. Being placed into a completely different area that you haven't studied since nursing school is really unsettling and uncomfortable.

As we approached the holiday season of 2020, I knew my turn to float was coming soon since my last rotation had been a few months earlier. Other units in the hospital had been short-staffed and my unit was floating at least one of our nurses per shift.

I had a conversation with my husband over dinner one night around that time. "I'm going to be so mad if I have to float tonight. I'm tired and just not up for it. Working on my own floor during Covid is bad enough, and I feel so burned out. But being out of my element will just make everything ten times worse. Ugh! I would give anything to not have to go to work tonight!"

My husband responded, "Babe, you've got this! I'm sorry you feel this way, but you are more than capable." His response was sweet, but nothing was going to make me feel better. I kissed my husband goodbye and headed for my car.

I stopped at Starbucks on the way to work and got myself a holiday drink to boost my mood (peppermint mocha, anyone?), but to be honest it didn't help very much. When I got to my floor . . . there it was: My name was written in red pen with a sad face next to it. It was my turn to float, and it was to a unit I had never been to.

My heart started pounding, and I became very anxious. It is never fun to be in a place where you feel uncomfortable, especially in a healthcare setting. If something goes wrong, you want to be familiar with equipment and procedures and have a relationship with your co-workers.

I walked over to the other unit, introduced myself to the nurses I would be working with, and started looking up my patients. I immediately felt a bit of relief. From what I could tell by looking at the charts of my assigned patients, it wasn't going to be a bad night. I started my first set of rounds at eight o'clock. I met all my patients and their parents, and everyone was kind. One particular patient stood out. Something about her touched my heart and made me smile.

At nine o'clock, I again walked around to check on all my patients and their families. As I entered the room of that little girl I had noticed earlier, she handed me a picture she had drawn. My name was in the middle, surrounded by little suns and rainbows. And down in the corner she had written, "Thank you for being so sweet and taking good care of me." My heart immediately filled with joy, my anxiety subsided, and I told myself, *Okay, I can do this.* That child was the light I needed at that moment. God was being so kind and reminding me that His presence was there with me in an unfamiliar place. Even the suns and rainbows she had drawn were a reminder of Christ's light to me.

God can use us to be the light to others in very tangible ways.

What made this incident particularly remarkable was that it happened around the time that the Lord had put the word *light* on my heart, as I explained in earlier chapters. I felt He was calling me to write a book, and I had been asking Him to confirm it—and to show me if the topic of light was the direction He was trying to take me. And then this night with this sweet little patient happened. As I walked out of her room, I was holding tears back and had goosebumps. Because the Lord often manifests Himself to me through my tears and goosebumps, I felt so seen by Him right then. He seemed to be fully confirming He wanted me to study light. I couldn't help but think, *God is so amazing and so, so good.*

That girl was the light I needed that night. This child's act of kindness turned my negativity around, and God used her to speak to me. My friend, *that* is what we can do for other people. With our minds and hands wide open, God can use us to be the light to others in very tangible ways. Through the rest of this chapter, we are going to look at practical ways we can learn how to love others as Jesus would.

BE A LIGHT

To be the light and love others, we have to practice the five elements of LIGHT: Listen with purpose, practice Intentionality, use Gestures, have a good Heart posture, and Talk with kindness. These are some of the things that Jesus focused on when He was walking on earth, and we can focus on the same things to be the light that others need. As you read ahead in this chapter, keep the question *How would Jesus live my life?* in the back of your mind. Now, let's explore each of these five elements of LIGHT in more detail!

LISTEN

Have you ever been in a conversation with someone and just after you tell them something important, their instant response is to compare it to something in their own life? You suddenly don't feel seen, cared for, or truly heard. Or what about the times you are talking to someone and their focus seems to be on their phone, their eyes are veering off in the distance, or they get distracted by their surroundings? Odds are you have had this happen to you in your life. But there's also a pretty good chance you have done a few of these to someone else.

To love like Jesus and be lights for Him, we need to become good listeners. Jesus was *the best* listener. He wasn't rushed, He wasn't distracted, and He wasn't trying to show how He had something similar happen to Him. He simply listened. He made other people feel heard and valued. We can love others so well simply by the way we listen to them.

Jesus was also interruptible. He was never so hurried that He wouldn't stop and do whatever the Father told Him to do along His way. This trait of being interruptible is another way that He made people feel heard. When we are talking to others, we must work on being interruptible rather than always interrupting. If we listen with intent and make the time to listen, we will begin to look more like Jesus.

INTENTIONALITY

Jesus's goal was to make God known. Therefore, He was intentional in everything He did. He was purposeful in where He went, whom He spoke with, and what He spoke to them about.

God is also intentional with each of us. He places moments in our paths and puts people in our lives for very specific reasons. He purposefully does things for us that are specific to our hearts' longings and will make us feel loved. After all, He knit us in our mother's womb, He knows our deepest desires, and He is intentional to love us in the way He knows we receive love. What a beautiful gift it is to be loved intentionally by God! That's part of the reason Psalm 139 is one of my favorites. I love it in all Bible translations but specifically the way it is paraphrased in the Passion Translation:

> Lord, you know everything there is to know about me.
> You perceive every movement of my heart and soul, and you
>   understand my every thought before it even enters my
>   mind.
> You are so intimately aware of me, Lord.
> You read my heart like an open book and you know all the
>   words I'm about to speak before I even start a sentence!
> You know every step I will take before my journey even
>   begins.
> You've gone into my future to prepare the way, and in kind-
>   ness you follow behind me to spare me from the harm of
>   my past.
> You have laid your hand on me!
>   (Psalm 139:1–5, TPT)

God loves us so intentionally and Jesus walked a life of intentionality, so we also are to do the same for others. Here are some actions you can do to be intentional with the people in your life:

- Text a friend and let them know you are thinking of them.
- Take a friend out to dinner at their favorite restaurant and pay for their meal.
- Write your parents a handwritten letter or card thanking them for what they have done for you.

- Say hi to a stranger as you cross the street.
- Smile at the unhoused person who probably really needs a smile.
- Let someone who looks rushed go in front of you at the grocery store checkout line.
- Know the love languages of your closest friends and do your best to love them in that way.
- Try to talk less about yourself when you are with a friend and let them talk to you.
- Take the time to think of each of your friends and do something you know would bring a smile to their face.

There are so many different things that we can do to be intentional with others. Not only does it bring joy to them, but when we serve others, it also brings joy to us.

GESTURES

We can say a lot through our body language without using any words at all. Have you ever had a conversation with someone whose arms are crossed as their foot taps on the ground? It automatically makes you feel like they have better things to do than listen to what you are saying. We walk away from that conversation feeling defeated and not loved very well. The way we use our bodies when we talk or when we listen matters so much. I doubt Jesus ever used body language toward someone that made them feel less than or unimportant.

The next time you have a conversation with someone, try to intentionally think about the body language you are using. Look them in the eyes, let your movements be calm, and keep your hands and arms in a place that looks open, not closed off. Pay attention to the way people use their body language when they talk to you. Notice what makes you feel seen and known and then try and replicate that when you talk to others. Let's pray and hope that people who don't know Jesus would know His love through the way that we love. That includes our body language!

HEART POSTURE

Proverbs 4:23 says, "Above all else, guard your heart, for everything you do flows from it." *Every single thing that you do comes from your heart.* So, how is your heart? Truly, how are you doing? Let's pause for a moment to do a little heart check-in. Ask yourself, *Where is my heart, and how is it doing?*

If everything we do flows from our hearts, we need to protect them from things that are unhealthy and rooted in worldly influences. As much as we want to say that music, movies, TV shows, and the things we partake in do not influence us—they do. What our eyes see, what our ears hear, and the messages we are taught will affect how we live and how we speak.

> **What we put in our hearts will greatly affect the way that we shine light in this world.**

I say all this so you can be aware. I want you to be cognizant of the words that your ears hear. Make holy decisions when it comes to what your eyes watch on TV or online. Be aware of the scenes and crowds you hang out around. Guard your heart against the things of the Enemy. Saturate your heart with the truth of who God is. If we learn more about God, see more how Jesus lived, and hear more about His love, His light will flow from our hearts for others to see. What we put in our hearts will greatly affect the way that we shine light in this world.

Talk with Kindness

What we speak, how we speak, and the tone we use to speak matter. It's not too hard to be kind to a stranger, but it can be really hard to always be kind to those we are closest to. Ugh, why is it that we snap at, say unkind words to, and use a tone that isn't loving toward those we spend most of our time with? This is an area that I fall short in and have to constantly repent of. I know I am not alone in it. You might be reading this right now and feel a big sense of relief, knowing that you're not the only one who has a tendency to say unkind words to your spouse or parent or sibling.

You know and I know that there is never a good excuse for using words that are unkind. But we do have to remember that, try as we might, we are never going to be perfect at speaking kindly. We are going to mess up. We are going to hurt others with our words, and we are going to be hurt by other people's words. What is important, then, is what we do after we have said those words. We may not be able to take them back, but we can apologize for saying them and repent to the Lord. If this is something you have struggled with in your life, you can also ask the Lord to help strengthen you to hold your tongue when needed and help you speak only words of life.

In Proverbs, it says that the tongue has the power of life and death.[1] Wow. Just one little part of our body can truly add to or take away from someone's life. I have noticed that the Enemy loves to make us think our words don't mean a lot. And when he gets ahold of us, he sneaks in and causes us to say hurtful things—

or begin listening to or watching things that are of darkness, which we then imitate in our words and actions.

Take a minute and think of the last kind thing someone said to you. How did it make you feel? How did it change your day? How did it change what you think about yourself? I am sure it only added to your life and made you feel loved. If you asked yourself those same questions about the last time someone said something unkind to you, I'm sure your answers would be very different.

Let's be people who use our words to bring only life. Let's be people who are bold and speak kindness over strangers. Let's be people who speak light with our words. Let's be people who show others Jesus because of how we intentionally try to reflect Him!

Why is this important? Let me answer by sharing a story of someone I met who came to know Jesus by the way she was loved.

WHY BEING THE LIGHT MATTERS

It was a warm night in September and my husband was hosting a guys' night for our church at our house. Since I am in charge of my church's social media page, I posted on Instagram that while the guys were at my house, I would be hanging at the beach, in case any ladies wanted to join me. I received a text from a girl I hadn't yet met, saying that she wanted to come to the beach. I gave her details on the location and time. Then something came over me that had to be from the Enemy. Suddenly, I didn't want to go; I had no extra energy to give, and I thought, *Only a few girls are coming, so I should just cancel it.*

I told my husband about these feelings, and he said, "Babe,

that probably means that you really *need* to go." I ended up getting in my car, and as I drove, I prayed and asked the Lord to give me the strength and energy to love on the ladies who were coming.

I arrived at the beach, parked my car, grabbed my blanket and takeout, and went to sit in the sand. I texted the girl I hadn't met yet and began to look for her on the beach. I saw her, introduced myself, and we began some small talk. I asked her how she heard about the church and a few other questions, and she explained she had been coming for only about three weeks. Then she said something I wasn't expecting.

"I just gave my life to Jesus a few weeks ago."

My mouth dropped, and joy filled my spirit. The Lord spoke to me at that moment and said, *This is why I have you here.* All my ill feelings went away, and I became focused on her and intrigued by her story. I asked her if she would tell me how it all happened. With open hands and an open heart, she did.

It all started when she was working out at a gym owned by a man who goes to our church. One day, she was lifting weights, and unfortunately the weight fell the wrong way and she broke her elbow. The gym owner went with her to the emergency room and sat with her there all day. After that, he and his wife continued to check in on her daily, until a week later when she needed to have surgery to fix her broken elbow. When the time came for surgery, the man, his wife, and their kids invited her into their home to stay with them while she recovered, since she didn't have any family here in the United States because she was from Brazil.

At this point, she didn't have a relationship with Jesus. She had gone to church occasionally when she was younger. Since moving to the United States, she had been searching for fulfillment and community in other things—things that were unsatis-fying. As she began to stay in the home of this kind family, she was in awe of the way they loved her and one another. She said there was something different about them that was contagious. She wanted what they had.

What they had was the love of Jesus. Because of the way they loved her and lived their lives, she decided she wanted to have a relationship with Jesus too. She accepted Jesus into her heart and completely turned her life around.

Her story encouraged my heart so much. This couple didn't try to shove the gospel down her throat. They didn't tell her all the things she was doing wrong. They didn't tell her to do this or do that. They simply loved her as Jesus would. They let His light shine through them to her, and it was contagious.

I drove home that night after the beach feeling so filled up. I was deeply thankful to the Lord for giving me the strength I needed. The Enemy didn't want me there. The Enemy knew what God was up to. Let this be a tiny reminder that the Enemy is out there to steal, kill, and destroy our joy. Lean on the strength of the Lord to fight against it. He will sustain you.

He wants to use you as His vessel to reach

people who need His love.

A few months after that beach night, while getting to know my new friend more, I asked her if she would share with me some specific things this couple did that showed her the light of Jesus. One of the very first things out of her mouth was that the man listened to her with purpose and intention. He looked her in the eyes, he wasn't distracted, and he was always asking her questions. She said she had never been listened to like that before.

Another thing she said was that she had never been served with such humility. She was not close with this couple before this incident. They had only ever had short conversations in the gym. And yet this family opened their home and offered to help take care of her as she recovered after surgery. They were so intentional about loving her and putting her needs above their own. They were being the hands and feet of Jesus to someone who was lost, and because of that, she found her way home.

What Jesus did through the love of this family, He also can do through you. His light is in you, and He is ready to shine through you. Through our intentionality, the way we listen, the way we carry ourselves, our heart posture, and how we speak to others, we are being the hands and feet of Jesus. We are becoming a walking reflection of who He is. God saw my friend and used this couple to grab hold of her heart. God saw me when I was feeling down and used a sweet little girl to be His light to me. He wants to use you as His vessel to reach people who need His love. Shift your mindset away from *How can I improve myself?* to *How can I love like Jesus?*

May the light we carry be so contagious. Just as my friend saw what this couple had and wanted it for herself, may our faith also inspire others who don't know Jesus. May people ask us, "What is so different about you?" and we answer with, "It is the light and love of Jesus." Go and be the light, my friend. Put these five actions into play in your life. Ask the Lord to help you do it. Ask the Lord to give you faith and joy that is contagious. Ask Him for His light within you to be undeniable.

ARISE AND SHINE

- What is one way you can be the light today?
- Who is someone that you could be the hands and feet of Jesus to?

13

IGNITED TO IGNITE

Spark the Light of Christ Within Others

I LOVE CHRISTMAS LIGHT displays! It must be in my genes. In fact, before I was born, my dad used to be the man with the coolest light display in town. One year he, my mom, and my grandma made and painted 101 dalmatians, and they got the whole cul-de-sac involved! You could say my expectations are high . . . and you wouldn't be wrong.

When I was a little girl, my favorite Christmas tradition was driving around our small town and finding the houses that had the biggest and brightest light displays. Mom would make hot chocolate to bring along, we would dress warm and cozy, then we'd hop into the car and turn on Christmas music. I remember the sense of awe as I stared at so many beautiful bright lights. They drew me in, and I was so mesmerized that I didn't want to stop looking at them. To this day, going around and looking at Christmas lights is still my favorite thing to do. I'm delighted when I see so many lights on a house.

I knew that when my husband and I got a house of our own I would want to put lights up for Christmas. So when we bought our first house, I begged my husband to put up lights outside while I went all out with the holiday decor inside.

As I was sitting on our couch admiring the tree I had just finished decorating, I felt the Lord show me that we are each like a strand of Christmas lights. When the lights aren't plugged into the power source, they are still called lights, but they aren't shining. They aren't doing what they were intended to do. It's only when we are plugged into Jesus, the all-powerful source, that we will shine. When we are immersed in who He is, we are able to live the life God intended for us and shine brightly for Him.

A city on a hill isn't one light shining; it is many lights shining.

Now, a house or a Christmas tree usually doesn't have only a single strand of lights on it; it normally has multiple strands. When a strand of lights is plugged into another strand of lights, the new strand begins to shine too. The overall effect of the lights gets brighter and brighter. The radiant light becomes undeniable and draws in everyone who sees it. I believe that is what God intended for us as communities. As we have relationships with those around us rooted in God's Word, our light will be completely undeniable. It will be like a city on a hill whose light cannot be hidden. This is just like in Matthew, where it says,

You are the light of the world. A city set on a hill cannot be hidden. Nor do people light a lamp and put it under a basket, but on a stand, and it gives light to all in the house. In the same way, let your light shine before others, so that they may see your good works and give glory to your Father who is in heaven. (Matthew 5:14–16, ESV)

The Message paraphrase offers us another way to consider this passage:

You're here to be light, bringing out the God-colors in the world. God is not a secret to be kept. We're going public with this, as public as a city on a hill. If I make you light-bearers, you don't think I'm going to hide you under a bucket, do you? I'm putting you on a light stand. Now that I've put you there on a hilltop, on a light stand—shine! Keep open house; be generous with your lives. By opening up to others, you'll prompt people to open up with God, this generous Father in heaven.

You are the light of the world. You are here to be light. Words directly out of the Light of the world's mouth. The light of Christ within you is meant to shine for all to see, not be hidden and kept to yourself. Jesus's light shining through you is what others will see and be drawn to. Jesus's light shining through you is how other people will be ignited to be a light for Christ too. You aren't called to be a light for Christ by yourself but rather with and in a community. A city on a hill isn't one light shining; it is many lights shining. It's many people rooted in God's Word, seeking to live a life like Jesus, and loving others as Jesus did.

OUR ULTIMATE CALLING

I participated in a cohort recently that was led by Christine Caine, and on a Zoom call she said something that really struck me: "We are first called to Jesus before we are called to something." In this life, it seems like we are always focused more on the "something" we are called to. We ask, *Lord, what is it that You want me to do? What is it that You are calling me to?* And we often lose sight of *who* we are called to as we pursue *what* we are called to. We are first called to Jesus. That is our ultimate calling. From there, we are then called to "go and make disciples of all nations, baptizing them in the name of the Father and of the Son and of the Holy Spirit, and teaching them to obey everything I have commanded you."[1]

Your calling is first to Jesus, then to go and make disciples. Knowing those two things, the Lord will reveal to you the steps He wants you to take forward and what He wants you to do.

What does it mean to go and make disciples? Making disciples means living a life that points to who Jesus is, and then inviting others into what you have experienced and come to know through Him. I can hear you saying, "Yeah, yeah. Go and make disciples that make disciples . . ." Because maybe you've heard it in church a million times and it's old news. Or maybe you are reading it and it terrifies you because your immediate thought is that you need to go preach or start sharing your faith on Instagram or start telling strangers about Jesus. Let's talk more about both of these responses.

Being a disciple of Jesus is something that should never get old and can never be overused. It is the greatest title we could ever receive because it means that we know and have a relationship with the greatest person: Jesus Christ. Making disciples is something that we are all called to do as Christians, and the Lord is going to call us to do it in different ways, shapes, and forms. Maybe He will call you to preach—if so, know He will equip you. Maybe you are to take a bold step and share with a stranger—if so, know that He will be with you.

Whatever it is and in whatever way He calls, following His

lead, even if it scares you, is better than staying silent. That light within you *needs* to be shared. That light within you isn't to be kept hidden. That light within you was made to shine so that you can be a disciple who makes other disciples. You were created to be a Jesus follower who helps other people become Jesus followers.

Not only are we called to disciple, but we are also called to disciple alongside other people. This is good news! You don't have to do it alone. Luke 10:1 says, "After this the Lord appointed seventy-two others and sent them two by two ahead of him to every town and place where he was about to go." The Lord called them and then He sent them out in pairs. He purposefully sent them with another person to share about who He was. Then in Matthew 18:20 we see Jesus say, "For where two or three gather in my name, there am I with them." Jesus sent out His disciples to make disciples, and God was with them because there were two gathered in His name.

There is power when two or more are gathered in the name of Jesus. (Yes, He is also with you if you are alone!) Getting plugged into a community is so important; it is where the fire and light of Christ are cultivated and grown. When surrounded by other believers, it's deeply encouraging to our faith. Like I keep saying, God's intention when He created the world wasn't for us to discover Him and keep it to ourselves. His intention was that we would share with others all of who He is. With other believers, our faith deepens as we see God actively working. And with nonbelievers, we get the privilege of sharing about who God is and what He has so kindly done for us.

Have you ever been to a candlelight service? If not, it's okay. Just try to picture this: You're in a darkened room. Everyone is holding an unlit candle in their hands. One candle is lit by a lighter. The fire on that candle can be seen by everyone in the room because as soon as light hits darkness, it shines. Then the person with the lit candle lights the candle of the person next to them. Then that person goes and lights another person's candle. Soon the room is filled with these candles that have tiny little flames, but those tiny little flames are now completely lighting up the formerly dark room. It's inspiring, it's beautiful, and you can't help but be filled with joy seeing all of the little lights shining.

When we gather with our communities, it's as if there are a bunch of beautiful flames shining in a dark room. We each show up with our flame, and when we are all together, the light is radiant. That light becomes contagious. That light lives with you wherever you go. That light could ignite another person's flame. And when your flame lights another person's flame, yours is still just as bright; it doesn't take away from any of the light that you already carry.

My friend, that is your calling: to be a light that ignites other lights. To be someone who has seen the redemption of the Lord in your own life so that the light of Christ within you is undeniable.

TAKE A STEP WITH THE LIGHT

My nana and papa are some of the brightest lights for the Lord that I know. They love the Lord with all that they are, the words of the Bible are written on their hearts, and they know the character of God so intimately. They are some of my biggest inspirations to be a completely sold-out follower of Jesus. They are in their eighties, and they moved into a senior living facility a few years ago. They were both healthy, both can drive, and they didn't "need" to be there. But for some reason, the Lord was leading them to live there.

My nana began to pray and ask the Lord what their purpose was for moving there. She also had what seemed like a crazy thought in the back of her mind; she wanted to start a Bible study, even though she hadn't ever done it before. Within two weeks of moving into the senior living facility, a lady came up to my nana and asked her if she would be interested in teaching a Bible study. My nana responded, "Well, I don't know if I am qualified to do this."

My nana's new friend proceeded to say, "It has nothing to do with qualification because God will qualify you. I feel in my spirit that the Lord has told me that you would be the one we need to lead a Bible study."

After my nana prayed about starting a Bible study, she sensed peace from the Lord and felt Him tell her that she would have to constantly rely on Him. God immediately let her know that this is where she belonged. This is where He wanted to shine His light through her. So she took a step with the Light, and since then God hasn't stopped shining through her. The Bible study has now been going on for a few years. Ladies in their eighties and nineties gather every Thursday to hear my nana speak on what the Lord is teaching and showing her. My nana had originally felt that she wasn't qualified, but the Lord shut that lie of the Enemy down real fast.

You are called to be a light igniter.

I have visited my nana and papa multiple times since they have been at this senior home and, let me tell you, *everyone* knows my nana. And *everyone* knows she loves the Lord because she cannot tell a story without showing how the Lord was at work in it. People have accepted Jesus because of the light that radiates from my nana. People have asked her to pray for them, even when they aren't sure if they believe in Jesus. She stewards the light within her in the most beautiful way.

My nana took a step of faith and trusted that the Lord would strengthen her. Not only has He strengthened her, but He has also used her as a vessel to shine His light and show His glory. My nana is a *light igniter.*

And, my friend, you are called to be a light igniter as well.

What is it that God may be calling you to take a step into? Maybe it's starting a Bible study like my nana. Maybe it's going to seminary. Maybe it's telling your family what Jesus has done in your life. Maybe it's sharing your faith more on social media. Maybe it's writing a book or starting a podcast. Maybe it's volunteering more at your church. Whatever is stirring in your heart and mind right now, if it aligns with who God is, then it is probably something you should take a step into.

The Lord knows where your light is needed. Where *His* light is needed. All we have to do is take the step. Go and be a light igniter.

OUR RESPONSE TO THIS CALL

The story of Mary being told that she would be the mother of Jesus is one of my favorites. Her response is humbling and encouraging and makes me aspire to be like her. The story of her being called to something impossible that would change the world forever goes like this:

> In the sixth month the angel Gabriel was sent from God to a
> city of Galilee named Nazareth, to a virgin betrothed to a man

whose name was Joseph, of the house of David. And the virgin's name was Mary. And he came to her and said, "Greetings, O favored one, the Lord is with you!" But she was greatly troubled at the saying, and tried to discern what sort of greeting this might be. And the angel said to her, "Do not be afraid, Mary, for you have found favor with God. And behold, you will conceive in your womb and bear a son, and you shall call his name Jesus. He will be great and will be called the Son of the Most High. And the Lord God will give to him the throne of his father David, and he will reign over the house of Jacob forever, and of his kingdom there will be no end."

And Mary said to the angel, "How will this be, since I am a virgin?"

And the angel answered her, "The Holy Spirit will come upon you, and the power of the Most High will overshadow you; therefore the child to be born will be called holy—the Son of God. And behold, your relative Elizabeth in her old age has also conceived a son, and this is the sixth month with her who was called barren. For nothing will be impossible with God." And Mary said, "Behold, I am the servant of the Lord; let it be to me according to your word." And the angel departed from her. (Luke 1:26–38, ESV)

Pay attention to her response: "Behold, I am the servant of the Lord; let it be to me according to your word." Mary stood on the truth that no word from God will ever fail. And sure enough, no word from God failed in her story or ever in the history of the world.

What if our response to our call to be the light of the world was "I am your servant, Lord; may Your word to me be fulfilled"?

I am assuming Mary didn't feel "qualified," but she knew who qualified her. She didn't let her past stop her from fulfilling the call on her life. She overcame any doubt or fear that she may have had by leaning on the strength of the Lord. She trusted that what God had in store for her life was better than anything she could do on her own. She chose to live boldly in the identity God declared over her—and that was as the mother of our Lord and Savior, Jesus Christ!

—◆—

You've made it through the book now, and my prayer is that you will go forth and have Mary-like faith. That you will stand more confident than ever in your identity as a child of the Light. And not only that you will stand firm and secure in that identity, but also that you will begin to speak that identity over others in your life. I pray that you will fully understand that the light within you isn't meant to be just for you. It is meant to radiate into every dark, hidden crack around you.

You opened this book for a reason. You kept reading for a reason. God knew this message was for your heart, for this time. I don't believe in coincidences but rather in holy, supernatural timing.

You were put on this earth to shine the light of Christ where only you can shine it.

You were made for this. You were created for this. You are capable in the mighty strength of the Lord. You were put on this earth to shine the light of Christ where only you can shine it. And you were put on this earth to ignite the light of Christ in those around you: those you don't know and those you will come to know. I am not telling you that it is the easiest thing you will do, but it will be the most rewarding thing you ever do because your reward is in heaven. I have confidence in you because I know the Lord is confident in you.

It's time to arise and shine. It's time to stop living in the lies of the Enemy and start living on the truth of God's Word. It's time to stop trying to shine the light on yourself but rather shine the light away from yourself and onto Jesus. It's time for you to shine the light of Christ so that all of the world may see and know the glory of the Lord. You've got this, my friend.

Arise and shine.

I am your servant, Lord; may Your will be fulfilled in my life.

INVITING THE LIGHT
INTO YOUR HEART

I WANT TO TAKE a moment to invite you to accept Jesus as your Lord and Savior if you've never done so. It's as simple as repenting of your sins and declaring your belief in Jesus. If you were once walking in faith but have strayed away and want to re-acknowledge your need for Jesus, this is for you too!

If you've read through this book, or skimmed through it to this page, and you are feeling the desire to say your "Yes!" to Jesus, I invite you to say this prayer with me:

Jesus, I want to follow You. I want to surrender my life to You. I repent of the ways that I have not followed You, and I thank You for Your grace. Right now, I make the choice to live my life for You. I want Your light to shine through me. I see that I am in need of all of who You are. Thank You for dying for my sins so that I can have eternal life with You. Help me, strengthen me, and shine Your light through me. Amen!

Picture me jumping up and down with you and giving you the biggest hug! Wow. What you just decided to do is *huge,* and I am so proud of you. What should you do now?

1. Tell someone! Share your decision to walk with Jesus with a friend or someone at a local church if you are not attending one yet.
2. If you aren't plugged into a church community, search for one near you on the internet or Instagram!
3. Journal about your decision. If you haven't read your Bible in a while, I recommend opening up one of the Gospels (Matthew, Mark, Luke, or John) and starting there!

INSPIRING VERSES

HERE ARE SOME OF my favorite verses about our identity as light. Lean on these when it feels really hard.

You are the light of the world. A city set on a hill cannot be hidden. Nor do people light a lamp and put it under a basket, but on a stand, and it gives light to all in the house. In the same way, let your light shine before others, so that they may see your good works and give glory to your Father who is in heaven. (Matthew 5:14–16, ESV)

For you are all children of light, children of the day. We are not of the night or of the darkness. (1 Thessalonians 5:5, ESV)

Again Jesus spoke to them, saying, "I am the light of the world. Whoever follows me will not walk in darkness, but will have the light of life." (John 8:12, ESV)

For it is you who light my lamp; the LORD my God lightens my darkness. (Psalm 18:28, ESV)

For you have delivered my soul from death, yes, my feet from falling, that I may walk before God in the light of life. (Psalm 56:13, ESV)

The night is far gone; the day is at hand. So then let us cast off the works of darkness and put on the armor of light. (Romans 13:12, ESV)

This is the message we have heard from him and proclaim to you, that God is light, and in him is no darkness at all. (1 John 1:5, ESV)

But you are a chosen race, a royal priesthood, a holy nation, a people for his own possession, that you may proclaim the excellencies of him who called you out of darkness into his marvelous light. (1 Peter 2:9, ESV)

For God, who said, "Let light shine out of darkness," has shone in our hearts to give the light of the knowledge of the glory of God in the face of Jesus Christ. (2 Corinthians 4:6, ESV)

Do all things without grumbling or disputing, that you may be blameless and innocent, children of God without blemish in the midst of a crooked and twisted generation, among whom you shine as lights in the world, holding fast to the word of life, so that in the day of Christ I may be proud that I did not run in vain or labor in vain. (Philippians 2:14–16, ESV)

Those who look to him are radiant, and their faces shall never be ashamed. (Psalm 34:5, ESV)

Arise, shine, for your light has come, and the glory of the LORD has risen upon you. For behold, darkness shall cover the earth, and thick darkness the peoples; but the LORD will arise upon you, and his glory will be seen upon you. And nations shall come to your light, and kings to the brightness of your rising. (Isaiah 60:1–3, ESV)

ACKNOWLEDGMENTS

ARISE AND SHINE is in your hands today because a team of people championed me, challenged me, and walked with me through the process of writing this book.

To my husband, Michael: You are my number one cheerleader. On the days when I doubted myself, you spoke the truth of who God says I am over me. From the day this book dream was birthed, through years of hearing me talk about light, and now seeing this come to fruition—you've only championed me through it all. I will never be able to thank you enough for your sacrifices to see me accomplish my dreams. I love you forever.

To my parents, Doug and Shelly: Your support and excitement for this book has meant the world to me. Being your daughter is the greatest joy. I would not be where I am today without your love and prayers. Thank you for only encouraging me to chase my God-given dreams. I love you so much.

To my mother-in-law, Bre: I remember sitting at a table with you on the campus of Point Loma, sharing with you this idea the Lord placed in my heart to write about His light. Thank you for your wisdom and encouragement throughout the entire writing process. And to Pete, your enthusiasm has been so kind. I am so grateful that you two are my in-laws.

Kaity, Darsha, Krista, and Stacia: Your stories are beautiful testimonies of the goodness and glory of the Lord. Thank you for your vulnerability. Your friendship means more to me than you'll ever know.

To my aunt Teresa and her best friend, Debbie: You two saw a gift of writing in me that I never knew I had. Thank you for believing in me and encouraging me to be bold.

Allie and Hannah: You two are the sisters that the Lord knew I needed, and I am beyond grateful for you both in my life. Your constant excitement and encouragement means the world to me.

To my literary agent, Teresa, and the whole team at William K. Jensen agency: Thank you for believing in the message of this book. Teresa, working with you on this book was such a joy. You are so incredible at what you do, and I am so blessed by you.

To Susan and the WaterBrook team: Working with you has exceeded my wildest dreams. Thank you for giving me this incredible opportunity and for wanting the whole world to hear about the light of Christ.

Daniel, Betsy, Will, and Eva: I love you all so very much. Thank you for your love and support throughout the years.

To all of my friends and family: I love you all dearly. You've had a front-row seat to what God is up to. Your belief in what God is doing in and through me has kept me going. Thank you for your prayers, support, and love through it all.

To my Words Are Golden fam, She Who Speaks Light community, and *you* my dear readers: *Thank you!* This book would not be here today without you and your support. I wish I could give you the biggest hug through these pages. My prayer is that this book would ignite you to shine and to ignite the light in others.

NOTES

FOREWORD

1. Centers for Disease Control, "U.S. Teen Girls Experiencing Increased Sadness and Violence," press release, February 13, 2023, www.cdc.gov/nchhstp/newsroom/2023/increased-sadness-and-violence-press-release.html.

CHAPTER 4: SHATTERED PIECES

1. See Genesis 50:20.
2. See 2 Corinthians 5:17.
3. David Guzik, "Study Guide for Isaiah 59," Blue Letter Bible, www.blueletterbible.org/comm/guzik_david/study-guide/isaiah/isaiah-59.cfm?a=738009.
4. Guzik, "Study Guide for Isaiah 59."
5. Genesis 1:27.
6. John Piper, "If We Were Created for God's Glory, Is God Merely Using Us?," Crossway, March 6, 2017, www.crossway.org/articles/if-we-were-created-for-gods-glory-is-god-merely-using-us.

CHAPTER 5: TRANSFORMING TRUTH

1. Crystal Raypole, "How Many Thoughts Do You Have Each Day? And Other Things to Think About," Heathline, February 28, 2022, www.healthline.com/health/how-many-thoughts-per-day#thoughts -per-day.
2. Genesis 3:1.
3. Jennie Allen, *Get Out of Your Head: Stopping the Spiral of Toxic Thoughts* (Colorado Springs: WaterBrook, 2020), 10–11.
4. Craig Groeschel, *Winning the War in Your Mind: Change Your Thinking, Change Your Life* (Grand Rapids, Mich.: Zondervan, 2021), 45.
5. Allen, *Get Out of Your Head,* 40.
6. James 4:8, ESV.

CHAPTER 6: CLOSER TO THE LIGHT

1. 1 John 5:14.
2. April Motl, "What Does It Mean That God is Jehovah-Jireh?," Christianity.com, July 21, 2023, www.christianity.com/wiki/god/ what-does-it-mean-that-god-is-jehovah-jireh.html.
3. Mark Batterson, *Draw the Circle: The 40 Day Prayer Challenge* (Grand Rapids, Mich.: Zondervan, 2012), 65.
4. *Merriam-Webster,* s.v. "worship," www.merriam-webster.com/ dictionary/worship.

CHAPTER 7: PIERCING PRAISE

1. Acts 16:16–24.
2. Chris Tomlin and Darren Whitehead, *Holy Roar: 7 Words That Will Change the Way You Worship* (Nashville: Thomas Nelson, 2017), 111.

3. Ann Voskamp, *One Thousand Gifts Devotional: Reflections on Finding Everyday Graces* (Grand Rapids, Mich.: Zondervan, 2012), 27–28.

CHAPTER 8: ARMOR OF LIGHT

1. Michael Golden, "An Offering," 2020.
2. David Guzik, "Study Guide for Romans 13," Blue Letter Bible, www.blueletterbible.org/comm/guzik_david/study-guide/romans/romans-13.cfm?a=1059012.
3. Leon Morris, *The Epistle to the Romans,* The Pillar New Testament Commentary (Grand Rapids, Mich.: Eerdmans, 1988), 473.
4. See John 8:12, ESV.
5. Lisa Loraine Baker, "What Is the Purpose of the Breastplate of Righteousness?" Bible Study Tools, May 19, 2023, www.biblestudytools.com/bible-study/topical-studies/what-is-the-purpose-of-the-breastplate-of-righteousness.html.
6. STEP Bible, Ephesians 6:14, ESV, s.v. "righteousness," www.stepbible.org/?q=version=ESV|reference=Eph.6&options=NHVUG. (Click on "righteousness" to see the word analysis panel.)
7. STEP Bible, Ephesians 6:14, ESV, s.v. "breastplate," www.stepbible.org/?q=version=ESV|reference=Eph.6&options=NHVUG. (Click on "breastplate" to see the word analysis panel.)
8. Ephesians 6:15, NLT.
9. David Guzik, "Ephesians 6—Walking in the Light and Fighting the Darkness," Enduring Word, https://enduringword.com/bible-commentary/ephesians-6.
10. David Guzik, "Ephesians 6—Walking in the Light and Fighting the Darkness."
11. See Ephesians 6:17, NLT.

CHAPTER 9: Keep Your Eyes on the Lighthouse

1. Psalm 91:1–2.
2. Alex Pattakos, "Guiding Yourself and Others to Meaning," *Psychology Today,* June 17, 2021, www.psychologytoday.com/us/blog/the -meaningful-life/202106/guiding-yourself-and-others-meaning.
3. Acts 27:10, NLT.
4. Acts 27:31, NLT.
5. See Acts 28:1–10, NLT.

CHAPTER 10: Protecting Your Light

1. S. Dixon, "Daily Time Spent on Social Networking by Internet Users Worldwide from 2012 to 2022 (in Minutes)," Statista, August 22, 2022.
2. Melinda Wenner Moyer, "Kids as Young as 8 are Using Social Media More Than Ever, Study Finds," *New York Times,* March 24, 2022, www.nytimes.com/2022/03/24/well/family/child-social-media-use .html.
3. Ephesians 3:20.
4. Most commonly attributed to Napoleon Hill.

CHAPTER 11: Fan the Flame

1. Dictionary.com, s.v. "complacent," www.dictionary.com/browse/ complacent.
2. Psalm 84:11, ESV.
3. Sadie Robertson Huff (@legitsadierob), Instagram, January 5, 2023, www.instagram.com/reel/CnDB4kOqYBl/?utm_source=ig_embed &ig_rid=5264571f-a591-40e3-aae4-126613314de6.

CHAPTER 12: **Be the Light**

1. Proverbs 18:21.

CHAPTER 13: **Ignited to Ignite**

1. Matthew 28:19–20.

ALLYSON GOLDEN is the founder and creator of an online ministry, Words Are Golden, and runs an online community for women called She Who Speaks Light. She is also the author of *Words Are Golden: An Inspirational Journal.* Allyson and her husband, Michael, partner in ministry at their local church in San Diego, where he serves as the worship leader and Allyson is the communications manager. When she is not writing and encouraging women, Allyson takes care of patients as a pediatric nurse and hosts people in her home.

ABOUT THE TYPE

This book was set in Caslon, a typeface first designed in 1722 by William Caslon (1692–1766). Its widespread use by most English printers in the early eighteenth century soon supplanted the Dutch typefaces that had formerly prevailed. The roman is considered a "workhorse" typeface due to its pleasant, open appearance, while the italic is exceedingly decorative.